A Teenager's Guide to

Character, Success & Happiness

Ultimate Goal Publications

www.stayinthecastle.com

(812) 665-4375

Cover Design by Rebecca Loewen

derekandrebecca@gmail.com

A Teenager's Guide to

Character, Success & Happiness

*Tough Choices That Will Make You
Insanely Successful and Outrageously Happy*

by Jerry Ross

Other Books by the Author

Stay in the Castle

Seven Royal Laws of Courtship

The Teenage Years of Jesus Christ

The Childhood Years of Jesus Christ

The 21 Tenets of Femininity

The 21 Tenets of Masculinity

Is Your Youth Group Dead or Alive?

Mountain Lessons

Grace Will Lead Me Home

104 Teen Bible Lessons

The Teenager's Guide to the Invisible Creation

The Teenager's Guide to Relationships

Did God Put A Book Inside of You?

Table of Contents

Introduction

1. Staying Simple is a Choice   9

2. Foolishness is a Choice   15

3. Wisdom is a Choice   21

4. Laziness is a Choice   29

5. Diligence is a Choice   33

6. Pride is a Choice   41

7. Humility is a Choice   47

8. Virtue is a Choice   53

9. Fearing the Lord is a Choice   63

10. Prudence is a Choice   69

11. Seeking Counsel is a Choice   75

12. Happiness is a Choice   81

13. Anger is a Choice   87

14. Teachable or Scorner?   93

15. Prosperous or Poor?   101

16. Blessed or Cursed?   107

Summary   115

*Character in a saint means
the disposition of Jesus Christ persistently manifested.*
— Oswald Chambers

Introduction

This series of Bible lessons is really about one thing: choices. During your teenage years, you will make some specific choices about the kind of person you will be. You cannot dodge these choices. Not choosing *is* choosing. The choices you make will largely determine the amount of success you will experience in life, and your success will determine your happiness.

Everyone wants to be happy, but few understand that happiness is the by-product of Godly character. So to choose happiness, you must first choose between your carnal nature and your supernatural nature. Only you can make this choice.

Godly Character = Success = Happiness

Carnal Character = Failure = Unhappiness

Your ultimate level of happiness depends on how successful you are, and your success depends on who you choose to become. If you choose to develop good character traits into your life, you will experience success, and your successes will produce happiness. If you choose to allow poor character traits to rule you, then you will fail at most things. Your unsuccessful life will soon produce unhappiness and frustration.

These Bible lessons will introduce to you 11 positive, Biblical character traits guaranteed to produce success. For every positive trait, there is a corresponding negative trait. Every teenager will choose one or the other. Choose wisely, because ultimately you are choosing between happiness and unhappiness.

As the excellence of steel is strength,
and the excellence of art is beauty,
so the excellence of mankind is moral character.
— A. W. Tozer

Lesson One

Staying Simple is a Choice

*One of these days some simple soul will
pick up the Book of God, read it, and believe it.
Then the rest of us will be embarrassed.
— Leonard Ravenhill*

Lesson Goals

1. Defining the simple man, foolish man, and wise man
2. Understanding why some young people stay simple
3. Understanding the costs of simplicity

Introduction

Unless there is a radical change of direction, you will one day be what you are now becoming.

This could be a good thing, or this could be a bad thing. The teenager, who chooses to pursue wisdom, is on his way to becoming a wise adult. The teenager, who allows foolishness to dominate his character, is on his way to becoming a foolish adult.

Will you be wise or foolish? As we examine what God says about each, may we allow the Holy Spirit to bring to light, in our hearts, the areas where we need work.

Defining the Wise, the Simple, and the Foolish

Matthew 7:24-27, "Therefore whosoever heareth these sayings of mine, and doeth them, I will liken him unto a wise man, which built his house upon a rock: And the rain descended, and the floods came, and the winds blew, and beat upon that house; and it fell not: for it was founded upon a rock. And every one that heareth these sayings of mine, and doeth them not, shall be likened unto a foolish man, which built his house upon the sand: And the rain descended, and the floods came, and the winds blew, and beat upon that house; and it fell: and great was the fall of it."

In the parable of the two foundations, Jesus identifies the wise man as "whosoever heareth these sayings of mine, and doeth them." He goes on to identify the foolish man as "every one that heareth these sayings of mine, and doeth them not." Notice, both the wise man and foolish man heard the words of Christ. Sitting under the teaching and preaching of the Bible has the potential to make you wise, or make you foolish. These two men could not claim ignorance! They knew what Christ said. The wise man valued the sayings of Christ and applied them to his life. The foolish man scorned the sayings of Christ.

Set three chairs in front of you. Line them up as if they were the front row of a Sunday School class. Now imagine the first two have students in them, and the third is empty. With that in mind, let's study the three main men of the book of Proverbs.

The wise man: A person who attends church, hears the Word of God, and obeys it. This man receives God's favor. Because he heeds the wisdom and warnings of the Bible, he inherits blessings and avoids destructive pitfalls.

The foolish man: A person who attends church, hears the Word of God, but disobeys it. Because he scorns

God's wisdom, he risks God's judgment. Wisdom would have protected him against foolish decisions.

The simple man: A person who does not attend church, therefore does not hear the Word of God at all. No one can obey what he has not heard. The simple man cannot draw on the wisdom and warnings of the Scriptures. Making decisions without the benefit of God's wisdom results in many mistakes.

Why Do So Many Remain Simple?

In America today, the level of ignorance concerning the Bible is astounding. The Bible is readily available and churches are everywhere. Why are there so many teenagers who literally have little or no knowledge of Biblical wisdom?

1. Teenagers are ignoring the invitation to come.

Proverbs 9:1-6, "Wisdom hath builded her house, she hath hewn out her seven pillars: She hath killed her beasts; she hath mingled her wine; she hath also furnished her table. She hath sent forth her maidens: she crieth upon the highest places of the city, Whoso is simple, let him turn in hither: as for him that wanteth understanding, she saith to him, Come, eat of my bread, and drink of the wine which I have mingled. Forsake the foolish, and live; and go in the way of understanding."

Wisdom's house is the local New Testament church. Every Sunday, preparations are made. The table is set, teachers have studied, the congregation has prayed, and the preacher is primed, but the simple have to accept the invitation to "let him turn in hither."

It takes a commitment to come faithfully to church. Sadly, many parents are not taking their children to church. So, a teenager has to decide on his own to make church attendance a priority. Those who refuse will stay simple.

2. Some teenagers, who do come, soon turn away.

Proverbs 1:32, "For the turning away of the simple shall slay them..."

Some teenagers do accept the invitation to attend church. But soon, the world's Sunday activities allure them away. Ball games, weekend trips, recreation, and family outings become more important to them than the wisdom they could receive in church.

Video game marathons on Saturday nights keep many in bed on Sunday morning. Many teens choose to sleep away their opportunity for wisdom.

3. Some teenagers love ignorance.

Proverbs 1:22, "How long, ye simple ones, will ye love simplicity? and the scorners delight in their scorning, and fools hate knowledge?"

What a question! Could it be that civilization has digressed to the point that it is now "cool" to be ignorant? Do people really believe that they are not accountable for the things they fail to learn?

What is the Cost of Simplicity?

Is not attending church and not being taught the Bible really that big of a deal? I mean, the old saying goes, "What you don't know can't hurt you."

Bible principles provide protection! Let's look at the cost of staying simple.

1. The simple are easily deceived.

Proverbs 14:15, *"The simple believeth every word: but the prudent man looketh well to his going."*

The book of Proverbs introduces you to 27 different types of people, some good and some bad. It identifies their actions and tendencies, and teaches you how to deal with each one.

A simple person knows none of this. So, he is ill-equipped to navigate life, and is easily deceived by the words of evil men.

2. The simple are short-sighted.

Proverbs 22:3, *"A prudent man foreseeth the evil, and hideth himself: but the simple pass on, and are pun-ished."*

The Bible also exposes our most dangerous enemy, Satan. We learn from the Scriptures how he sets his traps. Because of this, we are able to foresee what Proverbs calls "the snares of death." How foolish to have this information available, but refuse to attend church and learn it.

3. The simple become easy targets for sexual predators.

Proverbs 7:6-8, *"For at the window of my house I looked through my casement, And beheld among the simple ones, I discerned among the youths, a young man void of understanding, Passing through the street near her corner; and he went the way to her house,"*

The moral track record of an unchurched generation is tragic. The principles found in the Scriptures are designed to safely lead young people to the marriage altar, pure and chaste. The simple are ignorant of these truths, and become easy prey for the wicked man and the strange woman.

If you have parents that love the Lord and take you to church, you are blessed! Yet, you still have to make a choice. Every week, you will hear Bible principles. Hearing does not necessarily make you wise, but it will make you choose.

Points to Ponder and Discuss

1. How can I impress upon other teenagers the importance of coming to church?

2. How can I encourage more teenagers to come to church?

3. When new teenagers do attend, what can I do to help them become faithful attendees?

4. When was the last time I really thanked my parents for seeing to it that my family is in church?

Lesson Two
Foolishness is a Choice

Many men know a great deal, and are all the greater fools
for it. There is no fool so great a fool as a knowing fool.
But to know how to use knowledge is to have wisdom.
— Charles Spurgeon

Lesson Goals
1. Reviewing the definition of the foolish man
2. Exposing foolishness in our attitudes and actions
3. Exposing foolishness in the words we say

Introduction

Staying simple is a choice. Becoming wise is a choice. And if you grow up and live a fool's life, it will be because you chose it. Your teenage years are all about choices. Be wise in your choosing.

Am I In Danger of Becoming a Fool?

Hearing the Scriptures taught will prevent you from staying simple, but will not guarantee you will become wise. Every Bible-preaching church produces two types of teenagers: wise and foolish. What you become will depend on your choices. Will you listen and apply the Bible principles that are taught, or will you despise and reject them?

With the help of the Holy Spirit, every Christian

ought to search for foolish tendencies in their life. We ought to be willing to undergo a regular, spiritual check-up to make sure foolishness has not found a foothold in our lives.

Foolishness Can Show Up In Our Actions and Attitudes

Foolishness starts in our attitudes and then reveals itself in our actions. It is so much easier to see wrong attitudes and actions in others than it is in ourselves. Thankfully, the Word of God helps by shining a bright light on each of us.

1. It is foolish to ignore reproof.

Correction is a part of life. If you are too proud to accept reproof, then you are robbing yourself of the wisdom you can gain through correction. How do you respond when someone corrects you?

Proverbs 17:10, "A reproof entereth more into a wise man than an hundred stripes into a fool."

2 It is foolish to despise instruction.

Everyone needs to be taught. There is so much to learn in order to be successful in life. How foolish to develop a know-it-all attitude toward those trying to instruct you. Are you an eager and ready student, or have you developed a resistant attitude toward Bible teaching and preaching?

Proverbs 1:7, "The fear of the LORD is the beginning of knowledge: but fools despise wisdom and instruction."

Proverbs 12:15, "The way of a fool is right in his own eyes: but he that hearkeneth unto counsel is wise."

3. *It is foolish to treat mischief as sport.*

It is not funny to purposely do or say things that disrupt your Bible class or that show disrespect to the instructor. It is foolish. It is one thing for you to decide not to listen, but when you think it is sport to cause mischief that will distract others from listening to the Word of God, you have sunk to a dangerous level of foolishness.

Proverbs 10:23, "It is as sport to a fool to do mischief: but a man of understanding hath wisdom."

4. *It is foolish to make a mockery of sin.*

There is nothing funny about sin. It was our sin that nailed Jesus to the cross. How foolish to laugh or joke about anything the Bible condemns.

Proverbs 14:9, "Fools make a mock at sin: but among the righteous there is favour."

5. *It is foolish to be quick-tempered.*

A wise young person keeps his temper in check. A "short fuse" is a sign of foolish weakness. With God's help, anyone can learn to control his temper.

How do you respond to correction? Even now, as we are going through this Bible study, are you embracing the truth, being honest with God and with yourself, or are you just getting mad?

Proverbs 14:17, "He that is soon angry dealeth foolishly...."

6. *It is foolish to meddle in another person's affairs.*

The Bible warns against becoming a busybody. A wise young person learns to mind his own business. Don't become the youth group gossip. Every one of us has more than enough in our own lives to work on without deciding to stick our nose in the affairs of others.

Proverbs 20:3, "It is an honour for a man to cease from strife: but every fool will be meddling."

7. It is foolish to undervalue your parents. You may not always understand or agree with your parents, but you should always be thankful for them. It is foolish to disrespect your parents. Your dad and mom have a lifetime of experience, and a heart's desire to prepare you for life. Listen to their advice, and respect their opinions.

Proverbs 19:13, "A foolish son is the calamity of his father..."

Proverbs 15:20, "A wise son maketh a glad father: but a foolish man despiseth his mother."

Foolishness Can Show Up in Our Words

We spent some time examining our actions, so that we can root out foolish tendencies. Now, let's examine our words. Foolishness in our hearts will soon finds its way out of our mouth.

Luke 6:45, "A good man out of the good treasure of his heart bringeth forth that which is good; and an evil man out of the evil treasure of his heart bringeth forth that which is evil: for of the abundance of the heart his mouth speaketh."

1. It is foolish to hate, then lie about it.

If you are hiding a secret hatred toward someone, ask God to help you deal with the hatred. Don't lie about it, get victory over it.

Proverbs 10:18, "He that hideth hatred with lying lips, and he that uttereth a slander, is a fool."

2. It is foolish to slander others.

To purposely spread false rumors or unflattering truths about others is cruel. It is also foolish.

If you have to demean others in order to feel good about yourself, you have a serious character issue. Why not turn that thing around. Try encouraging others. Not only will it make them feel better, but it should make you feel better about yourself.

Proverbs 10:18, "...he that uttereth a slander, is a fool."

3. It is foolish to speak perversely.

Sometimes, young people decide that the way to appear grown-up or worldly-wise is to begin to talk per-versely. Cursing or talking nasty does not make you ma-ture, it makes you foolish.

Proverbs 19:1 "Better is the poor that walketh in his integrity, than he that is perverse in his lips, and is a fool."

4. It is foolish to quickly speak your mind.

Have you ever listened to young children talk? Many times, they embarrass their parents because they seem to always blurt out the first thing that pops into their mind!

Immaturity is hasty. Maturity stops and thinks be-fore it speaks. Learn to slow down and carefully consider your words.

Proverbs 29:20, "Seest thou a man that is hasty in

his words? there is more hope of a fool than of him."

5. It is foolish to speak proudly.

Boasting and bragging are signs of insecurity. Confident people do not have to talk about themselves all the time. Don't dominate conversations with stories of yourself. Learn to be genuinely interested in other people.

Proverbs 14:3, "In the mouth of the foolish is a rod of pride..."

Proverbs 27:2, "Let another man praise thee, and not thine own mouth; a stranger, and not thine own lips."

6. It is foolish to be contentious.

It is foolish to pick fights or start arguments. Many teenagers walk around with a chip on their shoulder. Stop taking everything that everyone says personally. If you can't learn to take a joke and laugh at yourself, then soon no one will want to be around you.

Proverbs 18:6, "A fool's lips enter into contention, and his mouth calleth for strokes."

A wise Christian guards against foolishness. He spends his life seeking the wisdom of God. Wisdom is the "principal thing!" Get it with all thy getting.

Points to Ponder and Discuss

1. Review the definitions of the simple man, the foolish man, and the wise man.

2. Of the seven actions of a fool, which are you the wisest at avoiding?

3. Of the seven actions of a fool, which are you needing to work on the most?

Lesson Three

Wisdom is a Choice

The chief means for attaining wisdom,
are the Holy Scriptures, and prayer.
— John Newton

Lesson Goals
1. Reviewing the definition and importance of wisdom
2. Learning the Bible steps to increase in wisdom
3. Learning the great benefits of wisdom

Introduction

The principal priority of your teenage years should be the pursuit of wisdom. Let that sink in. There is nothing you should pursue with more diligence than wisdom. God's Word not only contains the wisdom of God, it also teaches us how to obtain the wisdom of God.

Proverbs 4:5-7, "Get wisdom, get understanding: forget it not; neither decline from the words of my mouth. Forsake her not, and she shall preserve thee: love her, and she shall keep thee. Wisdom is the principal thing; therefore get wisdom: and with all thy getting get understanding."

How to Increase in Wisdom

God places upon us the responsibility of getting wisdom. He requires effort from us if we are going to be rewarded with His wisdom. The Bible is clear on what we must do in order to obtain wisdom.

1. Fear the Lord.

All wisdom comes from God. If we are to increase in wisdom, our relationship with Him must be right. The starting point for receiving both knowledge and wisdom is the fear of the Lord. A proper awe and respect toward our Creator is a must if we are to obtain wisdom.

Proverbs 1:7, "The fear of the LORD is the beginning of knowledge: but fools despise wisdom and instruction."

Proverbs 9:10, "The fear of the LORD is the beginning of wisdom: and the knowledge of the holy is understanding."

An old proverb states that a journey of a hundred miles begins with one step. The second step cannot be taken until the first is taken. This may not make sense to you unless you are actively involved in personal soul winning. God opens His Word to those who are willing to become laborers in the harvest field, and withholds many things from those who refuse.

Proverbs 11:30, "The fruit of the righteous is a tree of life; and he that winneth souls is wise."

2. Pray for wisdom.

The Bible clearly teaches us that wisdom is there for the asking!

James 1:5, "If any of you lack wisdom, let him ask of God, that giveth to all men liberally, and upbraideth not; and it shall be given him."

Near the top of everyone's prayer list should be wisdom. Daily, ask God for wisdom.

3. Cherish the Scriptures.

The Bible contains the wisdom of God, but it is up to each of us to mine daily for the golden nuggets it contains.

Proverbs 2:1-6, "My son, if thou wilt receive my words, and hide my commandments with thee; So that thou incline thine ear unto wisdom, and apply thine heart to understanding; Yea, if thou criest after knowledge, and liftest up thy voice for understanding; If thou seekest her as silver, and searchest for her as for hid treasures; Then shalt thou understand the fear of the LORD, and find the knowledge of God. For the LORD giveth wisdom: out of his mouth cometh knowledge and understanding."

A heart that seeks wisdom will be rewarded! Memorization and meditation upon the Scriptures will deepen our understanding and wisdom. A young person, who listens intently as the Bible is taught and preached, will soon obtain wisdom beyond his years. What you do with the Bible determines what God does with you!

4. Be teachable.

Nothing prevents the flow of wisdom faster than man's pride. In order to be teachable, we must be humble enough to admit that we don't know everything. There are many people who are older, and wiser, and willing to share with you the wisdom God has taught them.

Proverbs 9:9. "Give instruction to a wise man, and he will be yet wiser: teach a just man, and he will increase in learning."

Your attitude toward instruction will either limit

you, or propel you ahead of your peers. Sadly, many of your generation insist on learning everything the hard way. Learning from both the mistakes and accomplishments of those older than you will greatly increase your wisdom.

5. Accept rebuke.

Man's pride resists rebuke. However, receiving rebuke is a necessary ingredient in gaining wisdom.

Proverbs 9:8, "Reprove not a scorner, lest he hate thee: rebuke a wise man, and he will love thee."

Proverbs 15:31, "The ear that heareth the reproof of life abideth among the wise."

Proverbs 25:12, "As an earring of gold, and an ornament of fine gold, so is a wise reprover upon an obedient ear."

Right now, go back in your mind to the last time someone had to rebuke you. Just thinking about it, what are you feeling? How did you accept the rebuke? Do you hold animosity in your heart against the one who had to rebuke you? Were you grateful for the correction, or have you developed a victim's mentality about the incident? Have you spoken out against the person who had to rebuke you? How is your attitude toward rebuke?

Rebuke is a part of life. It is a necessary part of teaching and preaching. It is one of the duties of the Holy Spirit. It is the responsibility of your parents and teachers. Wise is the teenager who is thankful to those who love him enough to reprove him.

6. Seek counsel.

Every young person should select wise individuals from whom he can seek counsel. Your "multitude of counsellors" should be carefully chosen. Select Godly adults who will give you Biblical advice.

Proverbs 19:20, "Hear counsel, and receive instruction, that thou mayest be wise in thy latter end."

Proverbs 24:6, "For by wise counsel thou shalt make thy war: and in multitude of counsellors there is safety."

7. Go soul winning.

The theme of the Bible is the redemption of men. The Great Commission is a mandate for every Christian to share the Gospel with those who are lost. Many teachings of the Bible will not make sense to you unless you are actively involved in personal soul winning. God opens His Word to those who are willing to become laborers in the harvest field, and withholds many things from those who refuse.

Proverbs 11:30, "The fruit of the righteous is a tree of life; and he that winneth souls is wise."

8. Choose wise companions.

Show me your friends today, and I will show you what you will be tomorrow. Many a good young person has been corrupted by the wrong crowd. If you want to be wise, it is vital that you choose wise companions.

Proverbs 13:20, "He that walketh with wise men shall be wise: but a companion of fools shall be destroyed."

Proverbs 14:7-8, "Go from the presence of a foolish man, when thou perceivest not in him the lips of knowledge. The wisdom of the prudent is to understand his way: but the folly of fools is deceit."

The Benefits of Wisdom

There are great rewards for those who pursue wisdom. The wise man is the blessed man! Glory, life, favor, promotions, treasures, strength, happiness and success are just some of the benefits of seeking the wisdom of God.

1. A wise man will inherit glory.

Proverbs 3:35, "The wise shall inherit glory: but shame shall be the promotion of fools."

Glory in this verse is contrasted with *shame*. A young person who chooses wisdom will be rewarded with honor, and avoid the shame foolish decisions bring.

2. A wise man's code of honor produces a blessed life.

Proverbs 13:14, "The law of the wise is a fountain of life, to depart from the snares of death."

Notice the word *law*. A wise man lives by a code, personal laws of right and wrong based on Scripture. Because he lives by these laws, his life is prosperous and successful.

Joshua 1:8, "This book of the law shall not depart out of thy mouth; but thou shalt meditate therein day and night, that thou mayest observe to do according to all that is written therein: for then thou shalt make thy way prosperous, and then thou shalt have good success."

Proverbs 21:20, "There is treasure to be desired and oil in the dwelling of the wise; but a foolish man spendeth it up."

3. A wise man will find favor with those in authority.

Wisdom is noticed. It is in high demand in the work place. A wise and trusted employee will receive added responsibility and promotion.

Proverbs 14:35, "The king's favour is toward a wise servant: but his wrath is against him that causeth shame."

Proverbs 17:2, "A wise servant shall have rule over a son that causeth shame, and shall have part of the inheritance among the brethren."

4. Wisdom produces physical, mental and moral strength.

Foolishness weakens a man. It is like a cancer eating away at your character and your reputation. But there is a cure! Choose wisdom! Wisdom provides strength.

Proverbs 24:5, "A wise man is strong; yea, a man of knowledge increaseth strength."

Ecclesiastes 7:19, "Wisdom strengtheneth the wise more than ten mighty men which are in the city."

5. Wisdom brings happiness.

I am amazed at how unhappy the average teenager is. These same teenagers usually point the finger of blame at the people and circumstances of their life. Seldom do they recognize the true source of their unhappiness.

Foolishness comes with a price. I've never met a happy fool. Remember, this book is about choices. Choose wisdom. Choose happiness!

Proverbs 3:13, "Happy is the man that findeth wisdom, and the man that getteth understanding."

6. Wisdom is the best gift you can give yourself.

Proverbs 19:8, "He that getteth wisdom loveth his own soul: he that keepeth understanding shall find good."

When a teenager chooses wisdom, not only does he become a blessing to others, he blesses himself! Do yourself a favor and turn your back on foolishness. Embrace wisdom!

The priority of your teenage years should be the pursuit of wisdom. If you make it a priority, you will be in a minority. You will not always be understood, but you will be reserving for yourself a splendid life! So choose wise friends, follow wise leaders, and study the wisest of all books — the Bible.

Points to Ponder and Discuss

1. What is the difference between how the wise teenager views the Bible and how the foolish teenager views the Bible?

2. Review the list provided in this chapter under "How to Increase in Wisdom." Which of these are you already doing? Which of these are you going to start?

3. Of all the benefits of wisdom, which one provides you with the greatest motivation to pursue wisdom?

Lesson Four
Laziness is a Choice

There are men so incorrigibly lazy that no inducement
that you can offer will tempt them to work.
— William Booth

Lesson Goals
1. Understanding the danger of slothfulness
2. Examination of the attributes of the sluggard
3. To examine your life and eliminate slothful tendencies

Introduction

One of the best gifts you can give yourself, your future spouse, your future children, society and the Lord is the
discipline of a solid work ethic. Slothfulness will cause you
more problems, more frustration, and more suffering than
almost any other, single, character flaw. If you will learn to
work hard and work smart, you can succeed in almost anything in life. Remember, unless there is a radical change of
direction, you will one day be what you are now becoming.
Laziness must be confronted and fixed before it becomes a
permanent part of your character.

What Kind of Life Does Laziness Produce?

1. A Life Spent Under Tribute

Proverbs 12:24, "The hand of the diligent shall
bear rule: but the slothful shall be under tribute."

The life of a sluggard is not a desirable life. He will always be under tribute (someone else's rule). No employer is going to give a promotion to someone who will not work.

2. A Life Spent Expecting Others to Bail You Out

Proverbs 20:4, "The sluggard will not plow by reason of the cold; therefore shall he beg in harvest, and have nothing."

The sluggard will not work, so he is in need. He expects others to bail him out. A lazy man is always trying to borrow from others, and sadly, usually fails to pay them back.

3. A Life That Irritates Those Around Him

Proverbs 10:26, "As vinegar to the teeth, and as smoke to the eyes, so is the sluggard to them that send him."

Nothing is more irritating to a hard-working man than being around someone who is lazy. How irritating? The Bible says "as vinegar to the teeth, and as smoke to the eyes..!"

4. A Life Coveting Things He Won't Work For

Proverbs 21:25, "The desire of the slothful killeth him; for his hands refuse to labour."

He will desire the same things that other people have — will feel entitled to them — even though he is not willing to pay the price to work for those things.

5. A Difficult and Painful Life

Proverbs 15:19, "The way of the slothful man is as an hedge of thorns: but the way of the righteous is made plain."

Laziness makes life harder than it is – soon, living each day is like breaking through a "hedge of thorns." If you are slothful, that is the kind of future you can look forward to.

Attributes of the Slothful Man

There are several Proverbs that describe the attributes of laziness. How important to make sure that the seeds of slothfulness have not already been sown into your character.

1. Untidy and Unkept

Proverbs 24:30-32, "I went by the field of the slothful, and by the vineyard of the man void of understanding; And, lo, it was all grown over with thorns, and nettles had covered the face thereof, and the stone wall thereof was broken down. Then I saw, and considered it well: I looked upon it, and received instruction."

Solomon judged the man as slothful by the condition of his estate. His laziness had allowed his home and fields to become overgrown and in ill repair. Had the man been more diligent, he would have cut back the thorns and nettles and repaired the stone wall. All this required time and effort he was not willing to invest.

An unkept room reveals your laziness. Just a little work each day keeps your room neat and clean. An unkept yard is home to a lazy teenager. Is there trash and junk laying everywhere? Go out and clean it up! An unkept appearance, again, is a reflection of your character. Are your clothes ironed, hair groomed, shoes clean, and body bathed? Why not?

2. Excessive Sleep

Proverbs 6:9-11, "How long wilt thou sleep, O sluggard? when wilt thou arise out of thy sleep? Yet a little sleep, a little slumber, a little folding of the hands to sleep: So shall thy poverty come as one that travelleth, and thy want as an armed man."

Proverbs 26:14, "As the door turneth upon his hinges, so doth the slothful upon his bed."

Do you sleep more than is absolutely necessary? The Bible points out that it takes just a little excessive sleep, a little excessive slumber to bring about poverty and want. One hour less sleep per day adds forty-five additional eight-hour days of productivity to every year. Forty-five! That is a month and a half more time to earn money and accomplish goals.

3. Idle Time

Proverbs 19:15, "Slothfulness casteth into a deep sleep; and an idle soul shall suffer hunger."

Do you have a lot of idle time? How many times do you say to your parents, "I'm bored."? One of the main differences between the diligent and the slothful is initiative! The slothful man complains because there is nothing to do, while the diligent man goes out and finds something to do!

4. Need of Supervision

Proverbs 6:6-8, "Go to the ant, thou sluggard; consider her ways, and be wise: Which having no guide, overseer, or ruler, Provideth her meat in the summer, and gathereth her food in the harvest."

The Bible points out that an ant – an insect – has the character to work without a guide, overseer or ruler. If you cannot be trusted to be left alone to do a job and to do it right, then you are lazy. The diligent man does not need someone checking up on him every few minutes to make sure he is working hard.

5. Procrastination and Excuses

Proverbs 20:4, "The sluggard will not plow by reason of the cold; therefore shall he beg in harvest, and have nothing."

Proverbs 22:13, "The slothful man saith, There is a lion without, I shall be slain in the streets."

Proverbs 26:13, "The slothful man saith, There is a lion in the way; a lion is in the streets."

Proverbs 26:16, "The sluggard is wiser in his own conceit than seven men that can render a reason."

"It's too cold today, I'll do it tomorrow." Then tomorrow it is too hot, or raining, or something… always something! A lazy person works hard at one thing – trying to get out of work. His excuses do not even have to be reasonable! "Can't go to work today…. a lion might eat me!" The sad thing is, you could send seven men to convince him that he is just being lazy and they would not succeed.

Now is the time to root out tendencies towards laziness. Nobody owes you a living. Learn to work. You will feel so much better about yourself if you develop a work ethic.

Points to Ponder and Discuss

1. Review the results of slothfulness. Is that really the kind of life you want to live?

2. Have you ever worked with someone who expected you to do both your share of the work and his? How did that make you feel?

3. What is the average amount of sleep you get per night? Do you need to increase that or decrease that?

4. What is the one attribute of the slothful man that you most recognize in your life? What do you need to do to fix it?

Lesson Five

Diligence is a Choice

Be ye still men of might and vigour,
men who serve their God with diligence and zeal.
— Charles Spurgeon

Lesson Goals
1. To properly define diligence
2. To understand the make-up of the diligent man
3. To examine the rewards that diligence produces

The Definition of Diligence

    Proverbs 10:4, "He becometh poor that dealeth with a slack hand: but the hand of the diligent maketh rich."

    The original Hebrew word for *diligence* is defined: a pointed object used to bestir self, a sharp point, to wound, to make alert, determined, eager, alert, focused, to think, to plan to attack or to work with optimum efficiency.

    Webster's 1828 Dictionary: Steady in application to business; constant effort to accomplish what is undertaken, exertion of body or mind without unnecessary delay or sloth;   to give due attention; industrious.

    The diligent man is a self-starter. He is determined, alert and focused. He is industrious and looks for opportunities to advance himself. He is not lazy and does not make excuses.

The Make-Up of the Diligent Man

This man is worth studying! Let's place the diligent under the microscope.

1. The Hand of the Diligent

Proverbs 10:4, "He becometh poor that dealeth with a slack hand: but the hand of the diligent maketh rich."

Proverbs 12:24, "The hand of the diligent shall bear rule: but the slothful shall be under tribute."

The "hand" of the diligent man represents his work ethic. Because he is diligent to work, he prospers. Because he is diligent to work, he is promoted – he bears rule. He understands that excuses do not produce results. He stays with a job until it's done, and done right!

There is a great verse in Ecclesiastes that describes what the diligent man does with his hand. From this verse we are presented with 5 great Bible principles.

Ecclesiastes 9:10, "Whatsoever thy hand findeth to do, do it with thy might; for there is no work, nor device, nor knowledge, nor wisdom, in the grave, whither thou goest."

1.) "Whatsoever" – **There are no small jobs.**

2.) "Thy hand" – **Mind your own business.**

3.) "Findeth to do" – **Stay busy on purpose.**

4.) "Do it with thy might" – **Always do your best.**

5.) "For there is no work, nor device, nor knowledge, nor wisdom, in the grave, whither thou goest" – **Live every day**

like it is your last.

2. The Substance of the Diligent

Proverbs 12:27, "The slothful man roasteth not that which he took in hunting: but the substance of a diligent man is precious."

Proverbs 18:9, "He also that is slothful in his work is brother to him that is a great waster."

Because he works hard to earn what he has, his possessions are precious to him. Unlike the slothful man, he is not prone to waste anything.

You appreciate what you have to work to get, much more than you will ever appreciate what is given to you. It is easy to spend money that someone else earns, but when you worked for it, you do not just see the money. You think of the time and labor spent earning it.

You can give twenty dollars to three different teenagers and watch them do three completely different things with it. One will spend it. One will save it. And the diligent one will invest it, and turn it into forty dollars.

3. The Soul of the Diligent

Proverbs 13:4, "The soul of the sluggard desireth, and hath nothing: but the soul of the diligent shall be made fat."

The soul of a man is made up of his mind, his heart, and his will. The term "shall be made fat" speaks of robust health and prosperity. Laziness produces unsound thoughts and emotions and leads to unwise decisions.

4. The Thoughts of the Diligent

Proverbs 21:5, "The thoughts of the diligent tend

only to plenteousness; but of every one that is hasty only to want."

Developing diligence causes you to think differently about everything in life. The sluggard is consumed with what he wants, but the diligent man's mind is working on what he can do to earn what he wants.

Let me use an example. Suppose you are looking at a store in one of the typical shopping malls around the country. Five people can be looking at that same store and having five different thoughts.

One thinks of what he wishes he could buy in that store. Another plans to get a job in that store. The third finds out what it would take to run that store. The fourth determines to own the store. The fifth sees himself building the store and leasing it to the store owner.

Successful men and women think differently than lazy men and women. Because their thoughts tend to plenteousness, they figure out ways to prosper. You have to begin to train yourself to think differently.

5. The Heart of the Diligent

Proverbs 4:23, "Keep thy heart with all diligence; for out of it are the issues of life."

A man's soul is a trinity made up of his heart, his mind, and his will. The diligent man disciplines all three of these parts of his soul. He disciplines his thoughts so that they tend only to plenteousness. He disciplines his emotions, knowing they produce the issues of life. He disciplines his appetites, exercising self-control. What a contrast to the lazy man who desires to have, but refuses to discipline himself so that he can have the things he desires.

Advantages of Diligence

As you look back over the verses we have covered, you can pick out the advantages of being diligent. Diligence leads to financial prosperity and promotion opportunities. A diligent man or woman thinks differently about what they possess, and sees opportunities that the lazy man is blind to. He uses the same diligence to govern his mind, his heart, and his will. He thinks right, so that he'll feel right, so that he will decide right.

Points to Ponder and Discuss

1. What is a good definition of diligence?

2. Review and discuss the five "diligent hand" principles of Ecclesiastes 9:10.

3. What are some ways that you could turn $20 into $40?

4. Discuss some money making opportunities for teenagers in your area.

Lesson Six

Pride is a Choice

It was pride that changed angels into devils;
it is humility that makes men as angels.
— Augustine

Lesson Goals

1. Understanding the seriousness of the sin of pride
2. Learning the consequences of pride
3. How to have victory over pride

Introductory Statements

One of the weaknesses of youth is pride. Come to think of it, it is a weakness of most all humanity. It is easy for us to think more of ourselves than we ought. Most of us do not realize the depth of the sin or devastation it creates in our lives. Consider carefully what the Bible has to say about pride, then ask the Lord to give you a humble heart.

The Deadly Sin of Pride

1. It is a sin to be proud.

Proverbs 21:4, "An high look, and a proud heart, and the plowing of the wicked, is sin."

2. It is an abomination to be proud.

Beyond just being a sin, God classifies heart pride as an abomination against Him.

Proverbs 16:5, "Every one that is proud in heart is

an abomination to the LORD: though hand join in hand, he shall not be unpunished."

3. God hates the sin of pride.

Proverbs 6:16-19, "These six things doth the LORD hate: yea, seven are an abomination unto him: A proud look, a lying tongue, and hands that shed innocent blood, An heart that deviseth wicked imaginations, feet that be swift in running to mischief, A false witness that speaketh lies, and he that soweth discord among brethren."

God hates pride because a proud heart attempts to take credit for His goodness and graciousness to us. Without God's mercy, we would all be burning in hell. That is what we deserve because of our sin. For any of us to be puffed up with pride is an offence to God.

4. God expects us to hate the sin of pride.

Proverbs 8:12-13, "I wisdom dwell with prudence, and find out knowledge of witty inventions. The fear of the LORD is to hate evil: pride, and arrogancy, and the evil way, and the froward mouth, do I hate."

A mature Christian develops the same attitude as God toward these sins. Since God hates pride, so should we.

The Consequences of Pride

The Bible is clear on the seriousness of the sin of pride. What if we ignore that warning? What is the cost of being too proud to lay aside our pride?

1. Pride leads to the sin of scorning.

Proverbs 21:24, "Proud and haughty scorner is his

name, who dealeth in proud wrath."

Pride produces a scornful attitude. When someone begins to think himself better than others, he begins to belittle others. When someone loses his appreciation for God's goodness in his life, that person begins to lose his proper respect and awe for God. Pride scorns God.

2. Pride produces foolish statements.

Proverbs 14:3, "In the mouth of the foolish is a rod of pride: but the lips of the wise shall preserve them."

A scornful attitude produces foolish statements. Out of the abundance of a proud heart flows foolish words. Just as humility and wisdom are interrelated, pride and foolishness always go hand in hand.

3. Pride always leads to strife.

Proverbs 28:25, "He that is of a proud heart stirreth up strife: but he that putteth his trust in the LORD shall be made fat."

Proverbs 13:10, "Only by pride cometh contention: but with the well advised is wisdom."

Pride produces strife. When a man has a proud heart, he also carries around a big chip on his shoulder. Pride creates contention. It stirs up strife in a marriage, in a family, at the work place, and even in a church. Unlike pride, humility does not feel like it always has to be right, or always has to have its way.

Two of the greatest Christians in the Bible are the Apostle Paul and Barnabas. They were a missionary team, and God used them greatly. But there came a time when they had a disagreement of opinion. Sadly, it turned into a "sharp" contention.

Acts 15:39-40, "And the contention was so sharp between them, that they departed asunder one from the other: and so Barnabas took Mark, and sailed unto Cyprus; 40 And Paul chose Silas, and departed, being recommended by the brethren unto the grace of God."

If there is contention, it's because of pride. Pride caused two good men to separate. Too many times, pride divides people who should be able to serve the Lord together in unity.

4. Pride will eventually produce shame.

Proverbs 11:2, "When pride cometh, then cometh shame: but with the lowly is wisdom."

Pride will eventually cause you to say and do things that will bring you shame.

5. Pride will result in personal destruction.

Proverbs 16:18, "Pride goeth before destruction, and an haughty spirit before a fall."

Unless pride is dealt with, it will produce destruction. Marriages have been destroyed due to pride. Pride has wrecked family relationships, careers, even churches. If you want a life defined by destruction, hold on to your pride.

6. Pride places a man's entire household at risk.

Proverbs 15:25, "The LORD will destroy the house of the proud: but he will establish the border of the widow."

When a man insists on an attitude that God declares an abomination, he places himself in the path of judgment. Sadly, he also puts his family at risk. How much better to receive the blessings that come with humility!

Victory Over Pride

In order to overcome pride, we must understand the origin of pride, the stronghold of pride, and the cure for pride.

1. The sin of pride originated with Lucifer.

Isaiah 14:12-14, "How art thou fallen from heaven, O Lucifer, son of the morning! how art thou cut down to the ground, which didst weaken the nations! For thou hast said in thine heart, I will ascend into heaven, I will exalt my throne above the stars of God: I will sit also upon the mount of the congregation, in the sides of the north: I will ascend above the heights of the clouds; I will be like the most High."

Lucifer fell from Heaven because he wanted to be equal with God. Pride comes from an inner desire to receive glory that we are not due. Lucifer wanted the same worship God received, but failed to acknowledge that his beauty, his talents and his position were his only because the Creator had made him so.

2. The sin of pride is not of the Father, but of this world.

1 John 2:15-17, "Love not the world, neither the things that are in the world. If any man love the world, the love of the Father is not in him. For all that is in the world, the lust of the flesh, and the lust of the eyes, and the pride of life, is not of the Father, but is of the world. And the world passeth away, and the lust thereof: but he that doeth the will of God abideth for ever."

The world promotes pride. Humanism teaches us to take pride in what we are and what we accomplish. The

Scriptures teach us to give thanks to God for what He has enabled us to do.

3. The sin of pride is defeated by the fear of the Lord.

Proverbs 8:13, "The fear of the LORD is to hate evil: pride, and arrogancy, and the evil way, and the froward mouth, do I hate."

The teenager who stands in awe of God — His power and His grace — will understand that God gives us the strength and ability to do what we do. How disrespectful for us to want the glory that belongs to the Lord.

Points to Ponder and Discuss

1. Is there a "good kind of pride" If yes, provide a Bible verse or Bible story which supports your answer.

2. Who was right — Paul or Barnabas? How could their disagreement have been handled differently?

3. Why is God so offended by the pride of man?

Lesson Seven

Humility is a Choice

Nothing sets a person so much out of the devil's reach as humility. — Jonathan Edwards

Lesson Goals

1. To properly define humility

2. To understand the benefits that come with choosing humility

3. To examine the humility of our Lord Jesus Christ

Understanding a Misunderstood Quality

Humility might be the most misunderstood, positive, character attribute today. The world has packaged pride as something to be, well, proud of, and humility as a weakness.

The exact opposite is true.

James 4:10, "Humble yourselves in the sight of the Lord, and he shall lift you up."

The word "humble" in the Bible means "to make low." If I humble myself, I lower myself. Humility is not weakness, it is strength choosing to serve. If I was already low, I would not have to lower myself.

Pride lifts itself up. Which means a person who is proud is low, then with pride tries to exalt himself. Humility lowers oneself, which means the humble man is high, but chooses to take the position of a servant. Pride pretends to be strong, but isn't. Humility knows it's strong, but uses that strength to serve others.

The Benefits of Humility

James 4:6, "But he giveth more grace. Wherefore he saith, God resisteth the proud, but giveth grace unto the humble."

The Bible presents us with two options. We can live every day receiving the grace of God, or we can live every day receiving the resistance of God. God works **for** the humble and **against** the proud. Imagine living every day with the almighty, all-powerful Creator of the universe poised to resist everything you are trying to accomplish! How foolish to hold on to your pride.

One of the most foolish battles a man can engage in is a battle of wills with God! Ask Pharaoh how that went!

Moses, the meekest man on earth, faces the king of Egypt, at that time arguably the most powerful man on earth. Ten times, Moses delivers God's message, "let my people go." Ten times, Pharaoh hardens his heart, and in pride tries to defy God. It cost him his nation, his family, and finally the life of his son. That pride would eventually drown him in the Red Sea.

Remember, these lessons are about choices. Every teenager will eventually choose humility and grace, or pride and the divine curse that comes with it.

Humility Involves Your Spirit

Weakness feels the need to prove oneself strong.

Strength has the confidence to lower oneself to serve. Your attitude about yourself, and your attitude about others will determine your willingness to serve, or your determination to be served.

Proverbs 16:19, "Better it is to be of an humble spirit with the lowly, than to divide the spoil with the proud."

Proverbs 29:23, "A man's pride shall bring him low: but honour shall uphold the humble in spirit."

The Supernatural Benefits of Choosing Humility

God blesses humility. Proverbs teaches us that there are great benefits when we choose to lower ourselves and, instead, exalt the Lord.

1. The Humble Will Receive Honor.

Proverbs 18:12, "Before destruction the heart of man is haughty, and before honour is humility."

God determines who will be brought to honor and who will be brought to shame. So much of the Christian life defies human logic. The way up, for a Christian, is to first go down. And the fastest way to the bottom is to try to exalt yourself to the top.

As Christians, our duty is to exalt Christ. John the Baptist was a courageous and fearless preacher. He was sent by God to prepare the way for the coming of Christ. Jesus called John the greatest of all the prophets. What earned John such high praise from the Son of God?

John 1:19-27, "And this is the record of John, when the Jews sent priests and Levites from Jerusalem to ask him, Who art thou? And he confessed, and denied not; but confessed, I am not the Christ. And they asked him, What then? Art thou Elias? And he saith, I am not. Art thou that prophet? And he answered, No. Then said they unto him, Who art thou? that we may give an answer to them that sent us. What sayest thou of thyself? He said, I am the voice of one crying in the wilderness... He it is, who coming after me is preferred before me, whose shoe's latchet I am not worthy to unloose."

John 3:30, "He must increase, but I must decrease."

2. The Humble Will be Blessed with Riches, Honor and Life

Proverbs 22:4, "By humility and the fear of the LORD are riches, and honour, and life."

We live in such a materialistic society that it is hard for Americans to see the word *riches* and not think of money or possessions. Some of the richest people I know are missionaries who live on a foreign field with few material possessions. Humility contributes to a rich life — one that truly makes a difference for the Lord Jesus Christ.

Honor, riches, life, and grace await those humble enough to bow before God and seek His help. God looks for such a person to bless. Be that person!

3. The Humble Will Be Granted Grace

Proverbs 3:34, "Surely he scorneth the scorners: but he giveth grace unto the lowly."

Once again, grace is promised to those who remain humble. God's unmerited favor undergirds and guides the Christian who chooses to be a servant.

The Example of Our Lord Jesus Christ

Philippians 2:4-11, "Look not every man on his own things, but every man also on the things of others. Let this mind be in you, which was also in Christ Jesus: Who, being in the form of God, thought it not robbery to be equal with God: But made himself of no reputation, and took upon him the form of a servant, and was made in the likeness of men: And being found in fashion as a man, he humbled himself, and became obedient unto death, even the death of the cross. Wherefore God also hath highly exalted him, and given him a name which is above every name: That at the name of Jesus every knee should bow, of things in heaven, and things in earth, and things under the earth; And that every tongue should confess that Jesus Christ is Lord, to the glory of God the Father."

His entire earthly ministry is marked by humility. Jesus came not to be served, but to serve. Perhaps nowhere is this illustrated more clearly than in the upper room with His disciples just days before His crucifixion.

John 13:3-17, "Jesus knowing that the Father had given all things into his hands, and that he was come from God, and went to God; He riseth from supper, and laid aside his garments; and took a towel, and girded himself. After that he poureth water into a bason, and began to wash the disciples' feet, and to wipe them with the towel where-with he was girded...So after he had washed their feet, and had taken his garments, and was set down again, he said unto them, Know ye what I have done to you? Ye call me Master and Lord: and ye say well; for so I am. If I then, your Lord and Master, have washed your feet; ye also ought to wash one another's feet. For I have given you an example, that ye should do as I have done to you. Verily,

verily, I say unto you, The servant is not greater than his lord; neither he that is sent greater than he that sent him. If ye know these things, happy are ye if ye do them."

Ultimately, humility brings happiness. Are you proud? Too cool or too self-absorbed to serve God and others? If so, I can tell you this: you are robbing yourself of the greatest joy a Christian can experience — the joy of Christlikeness, the joy that comes from serving others.

Points to Ponder and Discuss

1. Discuss what Jonathan Edwards mean by "Nothing sets a person so much out of the devil's reach as humility."

2. Why does it take more strength to be humble, than to be proud?

3. Ponder this phrase, "God resisteth the proud." What do you think it means?

Lesson Eight

Virtue is a Choice

Virtue, morality, and religion. If we lose these,
we are conquered. — Patrick Henry

Lesson Goals
1. Contrasting the strange woman and the virtuous woman
2. Identifying the attributes of the strange woman
3. Choosing the attributes of the virtuous woman

Virtuous or Strange?

It is important that every young lady and every young man understand the character traits of both the virtuous woman and the strange woman of Proverbs. The strange woman is profiled in Proverbs chapter seven, and the virtuous woman in Proverbs chapter thirty-one.

Proverbs 7:1-7 "My son, keep my words, and lay up my command-ments with thee.....That they may keep thee from the strange woman, from the stranger which flattereth with her words. For at the window of my house I looked through my casement, And beheld among the simple ones, I discerned among the youths, a young man void of understanding, Passing through the street near her corner; and he went the way to her house..."

Attributes of the Strange Woman

The book of Proverbs provides us with an in-depth look at the attitude and attributes of the strange woman.

Sadly, Hollywood heroes and rock starlets are idolized by the average American, teenage girl. Most of these girls do not understand that they are patterning their lives after strange women.

1. The strange woman is a predator.

The young man in this chapter is identified as one "void of understanding." He is one of the "simple ones." This is who she targets for destruction. The first attribute of the strange woman is that she wants others to fall into the same shame and sin that now define her. Therefore, she targets innocent young ladies and simple young men, seeking to influence them away from God.

Proverbs 23:27-28, "For a whore is a deep ditch; and a strange woman is a narrow pit. She also lieth in wait as for a prey, and increaseth the transgressors among men."

2. The strange woman is a woman of the night.

Proverbs 7:8-9, "Passing through the street near her corner; and he went the way to her house, In the twilight, in the evening, in the black and dark night."

One of the attributes of the strange woman is her enchantment with the dark hours. The practical lesson for a young lady is this: night-time holds more danger and more risk of evil than the day-time hours. A wise young lady does not wander aimlessly after dark. She does not just "hang out."

The spiritual lessons abound. God is light! A virtuous young lady is dedicated to walk in the light of God's Word. The Bible truly becomes a lamp unto her feet and a light unto her path.

3. The strange woman dresses in the attire of an harlot.

Proverbs 7:10, "And, behold, there met him a woman with the attire of an harlot..."

Note it does not say she is a harlot (although, we certainly will observe she lacks moral character). What it does say is that she purposefully dresses to draw men's eyes to her body. Her attire advertises her disdain for chastity and purity, and suggests to men that she is open to seduction.

4. The strange woman possesses a subtle heart.

Proverbs 7:10, "And, behold, there met him a woman....subtle of heart."

The word *subtle* means *concealed* or *hidden*. Within her heart she carries hidden motives. She is deceitful and deceptive. This makes her untrustworthy. Nothing dims the countenance, steals the smile, and pollutes preciousness like deceit.

5. The strange woman is loud.

Proverbs 7:11, "She is loud..."

The Hebrew word translated *loud* is defined thus: *be disquieted, loud, mourn, be moved, make a noise, rage, roar, sound, be troubled, make in tumult, tumultuous, be in an uproar.* Obviously, *loud* in this verse means much more than the volume of your voice. A troubled, subtle heart boils over. The strange woman, laden with sin, most often tries to mask her misery with verbal bluster.

6. The strange woman is stubborn.

Proverbs 7:11, "She is loud and stubborn..."

1 Samuel 15:23, "For rebellion is as the sin of

witchcraft, and stubbornness is as iniquity and idolatry…"

The strange woman turns stubbornly away from God's original intent for her life. She wants what she wants, and there is no reasoning with her.

7. The strange woman disdains her home.

Proverbs 7:11-12, "…her feet abide not in her house: Now is she without, now in the streets, and lieth in wait at every corner."

Home, to the strange woman, is seen as a prison — a place from which to escape whenever possible. To a godly lady, her home is a sanctuary — a safe refuge and a sacred responsibility.

8. The strange woman is a shameless flirt.

Proverbs 7:13-15, "So she caught him, and kissed him, and with an impudent face said unto him, I have peace offerings with me; this day have I payed my vows. Therefore came I forth to meet thee, diligently to seek thy face, and I have found thee."

Many a young lady in our culture is patterning her behavior toward young men after the example of the strange woman! It is improper to lay hands on a young man, to flirt and kiss. A godly young lady would do none of these things. The strange woman speaks suggestively and seductively.

9. The strange woman has no respect for the marriage vows.

Proverbs 7:16-19, "I have decked my bed with coverings of tapestry, with carved works, with fine linen of Egypt. I have perfumed my bed with myrrh, aloes, and cinnamon. Come, let us take our fill of love until the morning:

let us solace ourselves with loves. For the goodman is not at home, he is gone a long journey:"

Our society is overrun with worldly women who think nothing of destroying their own marriages, or someone else's marriage. A virtuous lady views marriage as honorable, and would do nothing to put at risk her marriage or that of another.

10. The strange woman rejoices in the destruction of the simple.

Proverbs 7:25-26, "Let not thine heart decline to her ways, go not astray in her paths. For she hath cast down many wounded: yea, many strong men have been slain by her."

Once the strange woman has destroyed a man, she is done with him. She will eventually begin to target someone else. Her goal is to destroy "many." Destroying people becomes her perverted and profane mission in life.

The Virtuous Woman

Compare the attributes of the strange woman to that of the virtuous woman of Proverbs 31. Make a conscious decision to choose virtue over strangeness.

1. The virtuous woman is a wonderful, trustworthy companion to her husband.

Proverbs 31:11-12, "The heart of her husband doth safely trust in her, so that he shall have no need of spoil. She will do him good and not evil all the days of her life."

2. The virtuous woman is industrious.

Proverbs 31:13, "She seeketh wool, and flax, and

worketh willingly with her hands."

Proverbs 31:27, "She looketh well to the ways of her household, and eateth not the bread of idleness."

3. The virtuous woman is financially wise.

Proverbs 31:16, "She considereth a field, and buyeth it: with the fruit of her hands she planteth a vineyard."

Proverbs 31:18, "She perceiveth that her merchandise is good: her candle goeth not out by night."

Proverbs 31:24, "She maketh fine linen, and selleth it; and delivereth girdles unto the merchant."

4. The virtuous woman is well skilled in home-keeping.

Proverbs 31:15, "She riseth also while it is yet night, and giveth meat to her household, and a portion to her maidens."

Proverbs 31:19, "She layeth her hands to the spindle, and her hands hold the distaff."

Proverbs 31:22, "She maketh herself coverings of tapestry; her clothing is silk and purple."

Proverbs 31:27, "She looketh well to the ways of her household, and eateth not the bread of idleness."

5. The virtuous woman is tender-hearted toward those in need.

Proverbs 31:20, "She stretcheth out her hand to the poor; yea, she reacheth forth her hands to the needy."

6. The virtuous woman is modest and feminine in her attire.

Proverbs 31:22, "She maketh herself coverings of tapestry; her clothing is silk and purple."

Again, virtue is contrasted with strangeness. We learned that the strange woman adorns herself with the "attire of an harlot" — clothes designed to expose her flesh and advertise her immoral leanings. Virtue chooses "coverings." She adorns herself modestly. She chooses the feminine fabrics of tapestry, silk and purple. Virtue dresses beautifully feminine, yet safely modest.

7. The virtuous woman dedicates herself to making her husband a success.

Proverbs 31:23, "Her husband is known in the gates, when he sitteth among the elders of the land."

8. The virtuous woman has the strength to live by a code of honor.

Proverbs 31:25, "Strength and honour are her clothing; and she shall rejoice in time to come."

Strength and honor — what a combination! A godly lady lives by Bible principles, not baseless pressures. She is not swayed by the culture, the crowd, or carnality. Femininity is not weak. It takes great resolve and incredible inner strength to live a godly life in this ungodly culture.

9. The virtuous woman is wise and kind with her words.

Proverbs 31:26, "She openeth her mouth with wisdom; and in her tongue is the law of kindness."

Wisdom anoints her words. A godly lady passes laws concerning the use of her tongue. She remains silent if what she is tempted to say is unwise or unkind.

10. The virtuous woman is dedicated in caring for her family.

Proverbs 31:15, "She riseth also while it is yet

night, and giveth meat to her household, and a portion to her maidens."

Proverbs 31:21, "She is not afraid of the snow for her household: for all her household are clothed with scarlet."

Proverbs 31:27-28, "She looketh well to the ways of her household..."

The success of her husband and the care of her children are priority one! A godly lady manages well the home, seeing to it that the needs of her family come first.

11. The virtuous woman fears the Lord.

Proverbs 31:30, "Favour is deceitful, and beauty is vain: but a woman that feareth the LORD, she shall be praised."

Femininity lives in awe of God! A true Christian lady wishes to reflect in her life His holiness and His righteousness. Her reverential respect of God allows her to grow in knowledge, understanding and wisdom. It also shields her from foolishness.

12. The virtuous woman will be honored and blessed!

Proverbs 31:28-31, "Her children arise up, and call her blessed; her husband also, and he praiseth her. Many daughters have done virtuously, but thou excellest them all. Favour is deceitful, and beauty is vain: but a woman that feareth the LORD, she shall be praised. Give her of the fruit of her hands; and let her own works praise her in the gates."

The world may never understand, and the culture will shake its head in disapproval, but God sees and blesses the lady who chooses virtue! Her husband will praise her, and her children will rise up and call her blessed. In the end, to gain the approval of God is far better than the applause of a corrupt world!

Points to Ponder and Discuss

1. How are young ladies today being convinced that "strange attributes" are normal?

2. What are the greatest contrasts between the strange woman and the virtuous woman?

3. As a young man, which of these types of women would make the best wife and the best future mother of your children?

Lesson Nine

Fearing the Lord is a Choice

Fear God and work hard.
— David Livingstone

Lesson Goals
1. Learning to define "the fear of the Lord"
2. Examining the benefits that come with fearing the Lord
3. Contrasting the fear of the Lord with the fear of man

Fear of the Lord or Fear of Man?

Every young person will choose one of two ways to live. You will either live your life with a reverential respect and humble awe of Jehovah God, or you will live your life fearful of men and what they might say or think of you. The Bible as a whole, and the Book of Proverbs in particular, have much to say about the importance of developing a healthy and holy fear of the Lord. The Scriptures also warn us of the devastating consequences of living our lives fearing men.

Defining the Fear of the Lord

Psalm 2:11, "Serve the LORD with fear, and rejoice with trembling."

Psalm 33:8, "Let all the earth fear the LORD: let all the inhabitants of the world stand in awe of him."

Psalm 34:11, "Come, ye children, hearken unto me:

I will teach you the fear of the LORD."

Psalm 96:9, "O worship the LORD in the beauty of holiness: fear before him, all the earth."

Again and again, we are commanded to fear the Lord. Because God is holy and just, because He is perfect and pure, because He is all-powerful, all-present and all-knowing, we should hold Him in such reverence and awe that we would fear to disappoint or displease Him. God rewards the righteous and will punish the unrighteous. His love for us is displayed toward us in two ways: His willingness to bless our obedience and His promise to chastise our disobedience. Because of who He is, we both love Him and fear Him.

The Benefits of Fearing the Lord

1. Wisdom and Knowledge

Proverbs 1:7, "The fear of the LORD is the beginning of knowledge: but fools despise wisdom and instruction."

Proverbs 9:10, "The fear of the LORD is the beginning of wisdom: and the knowledge of the holy is understanding."

An old proverb tells us that the journey of a thousand miles begins with one step. The first step toward true wisdom and divine knowledge begins with developing a fear of the Lord. God grants to those who fear Him a level of understanding that is withheld from haughty men.

2. Secrets Revealed

Psalm 25:14, "The secret of the LORD is with them

that fear him; and he will shew them his covenant."

Honoring the Lord, with the reverence and respect He deserves, inclines Him to share His secrets with us. God's Word possesses immeasurable depth. God's Spirit possesses the secrets of eternity. God shares these secrets with those who fear Him.

3. Promised Protection

Psalm 33:18, "Behold, the eye of the LORD is upon them that fear him, upon them that hope in his mercy;"

Psalm 34:7, "The angel of the LORD encampeth round about them that fear him, and delivereth them."

In this crazy, upside-down world, it sure is a comfort to know that God is watching over you and yours. Special attention and protection are promised to those who fear the Lord.

4. Goodness Bestowed

Psalm 31:19, "Oh how great is thy goodness, which thou hast laid up for them that fear thee; which thou hast wrought for them that trust in thee before the sons of men!"

Psalm 34:9,"O fear the LORD, ye his saints: for there is no want to them that fear him."

Somewhere in Heaven, there is a warehouse full of goodness! God has laid up some wonderful blessings and provisions for those who fear Him. God loves to spoil His children, but reserves special gifts for those who hold Him in proper esteem.

5. Mercy Extended

Psalm 103:11, "For as the heaven is high above the earth, so great is his mercy toward them that fear him."

Psalm 103:17, "But the mercy of the LORD is from everlasting to everlasting upon them that fear him, and his righteousness unto children's children;"

Grace is God giving us what we don't deserve. *Mercy* is God NOT giving us what we really deserve. NEVER ask God for what you deserve! NEVER say, "All I want is what's coming to me." All of us deserve an eternity in Hell. All of us need mercy – not just for salvation, but throughout our Christian experience. A "great" measure of mercy is reserved for those who fear Him.

6. A Long and Meaningful Life

Proverbs 10:27, "The fear of the LORD prolongeth days: but the years of the wicked shall be shortened."

Proverbs 19:23, "The fear of the LORD tendeth to life: and he that hath it shall abide satisfied; he shall not be visited with evil."

A blessed and lengthy life is promised to those who fear the Lord. Life becomes a fountain of grace – a well spring of delight – when we exalt and embrace God for who He truly is. The years of the wicked are shortened, but the man who fears the Lord is promised protected and prolonged days.

A Warning to Those Who Refuse to Fear the Lord

Proverbs 1:24-31, "Because I have called, and ye refused; I have stretched out my hand, and no man regarded; But ye have set at nought all my counsel, and would none of my reproof: I also will laugh at your calamity; I will mock when your fear cometh; When your fear cometh as desolation, and your destruction cometh as a whirlwind;

when distress and anguish cometh upon you. Then shall they call upon me, but I will not answer; they shall seek me early, but they shall not find me: For that they hated knowledge, and did not choose the fear of the LORD: They would none of my counsel: they despised all my reproof. Therefore shall they eat of the fruit of their own way, and be filled with their own devices."

The fear of the Lord is a choice. God wants us to choose to fear Him. It takes humility to recognize God for who He truly is. To stand in awe of His holiness and power and to bow to His grace and glory — these things a man chooses or refuses. When a man in his pride chooses to withhold from God the reverence and respect that He deserves, he sets himself up for dire consequences. As one man said, "God may not make you fear Him, but He can make you wish that you had!"

The Fear of Man

Proverbs 29:25, "The fear of man bringeth a snare: but whoso putteth his trust in the LORD shall be safe."

Instead of fearing God, many fall into the snare of fearing men. This is especially true of young people. It is easy for you to succumb to peer pressure. Peer pressure is really just fear pressure! Teenagers are afraid they will not be accepted, or will be made fun of by their peers. To be accepted, this fear often makes them do things they shouldn't. Soon they lose their own self, and instead become puppets controlled by the culture and the wrong crowd.

It is a great day in a young person's life when he trades in his fear of men for the fear of the Lord. Betraying God in order to please some carnal friends leaves you empty and ashamed. Who cares what this world thinks! Live to please the Lord, and stop being controlled by opinions of mortals.

Psalm 27:1-3, " The LORD is my light and my salvation; whom shall I fear? the LORD is the strength of my life; of whom shall I be afraid?... Though an host should encamp against me, my heart shall not fear: though war should rise against me, in this will I be confident."

Psalm 118:6, "The LORD is on my side; I will not fear: what can man do unto me?"

Hebrews 13:5-6, "Let your conversation be without covetousness; and be content with such things as ye have: for he hath said, I will never leave thee, nor forsake thee. So that we may boldly say, The Lord is my helper, and I will not fear what man shall do unto me."

Points to Ponder and Discuss:

1. Discuss the saying "Peer pressure is really just fear pressure."

2. Give an instance where you had to choose between fearing the Lord or fearing what men might say or do.

3. How did Peter and John respond to those who tried to silence them through intimidation? (Acts 4:15-22)

Lesson Ten

Prudence is a Choice

*I think Christians fail so often to get answers to their
prayers because they do not wait long enough on God.*
— *E. M. Bounds*

Lesson Goals
1. To properly define prudence
2. To implement prudence when making decisions
3. To be prudent in our choice of companions

Going 75 in a 50 MPH Zone

For you teens who have your driver's license, have
you ever gotten behind an elderly person who was carefully
going the speed limit? How long did it take you to get frus-
trated with him? How long before you looked for a chance
to pass him? Here is the question: what are you paying per
month in car insurance, and what is he paying?

Why do 16-year-old drivers often pay three times as
much for car insurance than responsible adults? Because
you are statistically more likely to be in an accident.

One of the weaknesses of youth is haste. Young
people are always in a hurry! There is merit in learning to
slow down. It takes maturity to slow down – to calm your
emotions, control your actions, and collect your faculties.
Focusing your soul so that you think the right thoughts, feel
the right emotions, say the right things, and make the right
decisions requires an attribute that the Bible calls PRU-

DENCE. It is the antithesis of haste, and it will prevent you from making life-altering mistakes.

The Prudent Man Insulates Himself from Mistakes

Haste makes waste. It also leads to some heart-breaking mistakes.

1. Slow Down and Gather Before You Decide

Proverbs 18:15, "The heart of the prudent getteth knowledge; and the ear of the wise seeketh knowledge."

Proverbs 13:16, "Every prudent man dealeth with knowledge: but a fool layeth open his folly."

Proverbs 14:18, "The simple inherit folly: but the prudent are crowned with knowledge."

There are many decisions that await you in life. Always take the time to gather all of the knowledge you can before making a decision. The prudent man takes the time to research a situation before making a final decision. He gathers knowledge, then makes a wise decision based on the knowledge he has collected.

Proverbs 8:12-13, "I wisdom dwell with prudence, and find out knowledge of witty inventions. He that answereth a matter before he heareth it, it is folly and shame unto him."

Proverbs 14:15, "The simple believeth every word: but the prudent man looketh well to his going."

A trusting teenager has to understand that not all people are to be trusted. Many people spend their lives manipulating others. They create "witty inventions" – evil plans or mischievous devices. They love to create drama by spreading gossip, and telling half-truths, and getting others caught up in their foolishness.

The prudent teenager learns to "find out knowledge of witty inventions." He makes sure he gets all the facts before drawing any conclusions. Remember, there are ALWAYS two sides to any story. If you have only heard one side, you are in no position to make a judgment. Never answer a matter before you hear it – all of it! If you do, the Bible warns that it will be "folly and shame" unto you.

2. Slow Down and Think Before You Speak

Proverbs 29:20, "Seest thou a man that is hasty in his words? there is more hope of a fool than of him."

Ecclesiastes 5:2, "Be not rash with thy mouth, and let not thine heart be hasty to utter any thing before God: for God is in heaven, and thou upon earth: therefore let thy words be few."

James 1:19, "Wherefore, my beloved brethren, let every man be swift to hear, slow to speak, slow to wrath:"

Notice the stern warnings contained in these Scriptures! Be wise and take heed to God's instruction. Slow down! Think! Don't say the first thing that pops into your head. A mark of maturity is to stop and think before you speak.

3. Slow Down and Look Before You Proceed

Proverbs 14:15, "The simple believeth every word: but the prudent man looketh well to his going."

Proverbs 22:3, "A prudent man foreseeth the evil, and hideth himself: but the simple pass on, and are punished."

Proverbs 27:12, "A prudent man foreseeth the evil, and hideth himself; but the simple pass on, and are punished."

One of the most important character traits to develop is ALERTNESS. Young men, you will one day be the protector of your family. Young lady, you need to develop "momma radar" now. Learn to be aware of your surroundings. It is far better to avoid a problem than to have to deal with a problem.

Also, the prudent man avoids temptation. Jesus taught us to pray "lead us not into temptation, but deliver us from evil." It is far wiser to foresee evil and avoid it, than it is to constantly face temptation. No matter how spiritually strong you might think you are, it is foolish to consistently put yourself in harm's way.

4. Slow Down and Breathe Before You Get Angry

Proverbs 12:16, "A fool's wrath is presently known: but a prudent man covereth shame." Proverbs 14:29, "He that is slow to wrath is of great understanding: but he that is hasty of spirit exalteth folly."

James 1:19-20, "Wherefore, my beloved brethren, let every man be swift to hear, slow to speak, slow to wrath: For the wrath of man worketh not the righteousness of God."

If you have a short fuse, you have a big problem. It is something that God can help you with, but you need to take it seriously. A Christian teenager needs to learn how to control his temper. Wrath will do more to destroy the relationships in your life than almost any other thing.

Breathe! Count to ten. Take a walk. Whatever you have to do, but you must learn to control your temper. If you are constantly losing your temper over little, silly things, you need to honestly ask yourself a question: What are you really angry about? Talk to your pastor, and get some help.

The Prudent Man Chooses Wise Companions

Show me your friends today, and I will tell you what you will someday be.

1. Slow Down and Examine People Before You Choose a Friend

Proverbs 14:7-8, "Go from the presence of a foolish man, when thou perceivest not in him the lips of knowledge. The wisdom of the prudent is to understand his way: but the folly of fools is deceit."

A prudent young person chooses his companions wisely. Go back and review the character traits of the foolish man (Lesson One). Learn to watch people. Judge them by their words and by their actions. Yes, you heard it right, judge them. Examine carefully the words of Christ.

Matthew 7:16-20, "Ye shall know them by their fruits. Do men gather grapes of thorns, or figs of thistles? Even so every good tree bringeth forth good fruit; but a corrupt tree bringeth forth evil fruit. A good tree cannot bring forth evil fruit, neither can a corrupt tree bring forth good fruit.... Wherefore by their fruits ye shall know them."

Choose carefully your friends. Choose correctly and you will be better for it. Get it wrong and they will destroy you.

Proverbs 13:20, "He that walketh with wise men shall be wise: but a companion of fools shall be destroyed."

2. Slow Down and Think Before You Pop the Question

Proverbs 19:14, "House and riches are the inheritance of fathers: and a prudent wife is from the LORD."

Young men, study carefully the character trait of prudence. If you do not recognize it in a young lady, walk away. That young lady is not the one the Lord has for you. A prudent wife is from the Lord.

Young lady, study carefully the character trait of prudence. If you fail to develop this trait, you will be more of a burden to a young man than a blessing. By the way, this is a two-way street. The young man you one day marry — for your sake — I hope, proves to be a prudent young man.

Points to Ponder and Discuss

1. Describe the differences between a prudent teenager and a hasty teenager in how they would buy a vehicle.

2. Has there been a time in your life where you made a hasty decision and later regretted it?

3. In what way does Jesus encourage prudence in Matthew 14:25-33?

Lesson Eleven

Seeking Counsel is a Choice

A prudent question is one-half of wisdom.
— Francis Bacon

Lesson Goals
1. To understand the importance of seeking counsel
2. To understand to whom we should go for counsel
3. To understand the cost of not seeking counsel

Proverbs 13:10, "Only by pride cometh contention: but with the well advised is wisdom."

Proverbs 15:22, "Without counsel purposes are disappointed: but in the multitude of counsellors they are established."

Seeking Counsel is a Choice

One of the ways of avoiding disappointments in life is to seek counsel before setting out on any endeavor. There are people who have already traveled the road you are considering and have already succeeded at the task ahead of you. How foolish not to sit down with those people and glean some wisdom! Only a fool insists on learning everything the hard way. The Bible has much to say about the importance of seeking good advice, as well as the consequences of not doing so.

Some say "experience is the best teacher." They are

wrong. Someone else's experience is the best teacher.

Counsel, as used in the Bible, is defined as *secret or private consultation*. It is the act of seeking out someone who is wiser in a specific area than you are, and getting his or her advice.

When Should You Seek Counsel?

Proverbs 19:20, "Hear counsel, and receive instruction, that thou mayest be wise in thy latter end."

You should seek counsel when you need to borrow knowledge, understanding, or wisdom from someone. Counsel is seeking practical advice from someone who has more knowledge, understanding and wisdom about a subject than you do.

1. Seek counsel when facing a difficult decision.

Find someone who has had to make a similar decision in life, and pick their brain.

2. Seek counsel when you are struggling in an area of your life.

Find someone who is successful in the area in which you are struggling, and glean from them understanding.

3. Seek counsel when you need extra wisdom in dealing with a difficult circumstance in your life.

Find someone with a depth of Bible knowledge and ask them to share with you Bible principles that will help you handle the situation wisely.

Seeking counsel requires a level of humility that few young people seem to possess. If you are convinced that

NO ONE has more knowledge, more understanding, or more wisdom than you do, then you will never seek counsel. You are also a fool.

Proverbs 12:15, "The way of a fool is right in his own eyes: but he that hearkeneth unto counsel is wise."

From Whom Should You Seek Counsel?

1. Never seek counsel from the ungodly, from those given to sinfulness, or from a scorner.

If you insist on doing so, you will lose the blessing of God upon your life. There is godly wisdom, and then there is worldly wisdom. Always seek wisdom that is based on the principles and precepts of the Bible.

Psalm 1:1-3, "Blessed is the man that walketh not in the counsel of the ungodly, nor standeth in the way of sinners, nor sitteth in the seat of the scornful. But his delight is in the law of the LORD; and in his law doth he meditate day and night. And he shall be like a tree planted by the rivers of water, that bringeth forth his fruit in his season; his leaf also shall not wither; and whatsoever he doeth shall prosper."

1 Corinthians 2:6-7, "Howbeit we speak wisdom among them that are perfect: yet not the wisdom of this world, nor of the princes of this world, that come to nought: But we speak the wisdom of God in a mystery, even the hidden wisdom, which God ordained before the world unto our glory:"

Proverbs 19:27, "Cease, my son, to hear the instruction that causeth to err from the words of knowledge."

2. Seek counsel from your parents.

If you are blessed with godly parents, you should seek their counsel above all others. Outside of God Almighty, no one knows you better or loves you more. Young people who keep a tender heart and a teachable spirit toward their parents will be rewarded by God.

Proverbs 1:8, "My son, hear the instruction of thy father, and forsake not the law of thy mother:"

Proverbs 4:1, "Hear, ye children, the instruction of a father, and attend to know understanding."

Proverbs 17:25, "A foolish son is a grief to his father, and bitterness to her that bare him."

Proverbs 19:26, "He that wasteth his father, and chaseth away his mother, is a son that causeth shame, and bringeth reproach."

Proverbs 30:17, "The eye that mocketh at his father, and despiseth to obey his mother, the ravens of the valley shall pick it out, and the young eagles shall eat it."

3. Seek counsel from those who possess the specific knowledge you need.

The Bible encourages all of us to have a "multitude of counselors." It never hurts to get a second opinion. Two or three different people who are all basing their counsel on Bible principles will all give you very similar advice.

I do believe that the "multitude of counselors" mentioned also speaks of expertise. The reason we need more than one counselor is that different people have different levels of knowledge and wisdom on different subjects. For instance, if you are buying your first car, you might want to talk to a Christian mechanic before making a final decision.

However, he might not be the same person you would go to for medical advice. Some men are very good with finances, and their knowledge and wisdom on money matters should be sought. Another godly man might have an exceptionally good marriage and would be a good source for marital advice.

Seeking advice from a variety of godly men and women, who are successful in a variety of different areas, helps to ensure your own success. Their counsel will provide you with safety and ensure that your course of action will be established. It will also prevent failure, loss and disappointment.

Proverbs 11:14, "Where no counsel is, the people fall: but in the multitude of counsellors there is safety."

Proverbs 15:22, "Without counsel purposes are disappointed: but in the multitude of counsellors they are established."

Proverbs 24:6, "For by wise counsel thou shalt make thy war: and in multitude of counsellors there is safety."

Why seek counsel if I firmly believe I already know what to do?

Don't miss what I am about to say. The number one reason for getting counsel is to protect you from yourself! All of us at times want to do something, buy something, or go somewhere that we know down deep we should not. It is amazing how we can justify a potentially bad decision. Counsel protects us from our own heart.

Proverbs 19:21, "There are many devices in a

man's heart; nevertheless the counsel of the LORD, that shall stand."

Proverbs 28:26, "He that trusteth in his own heart is a fool: but whoso walketh wisely, he shall be delivered."

Seeking counsel requires humility. Its positive benefits are undeniable. God has placed wise and godly people in your life – learn all you can from them! Wise counsel will contribute to your success and will provide safety from disappointments and failure.

Points to Ponder and Discuss

1. What does it mean to seek counsel?

2. What types of people would make poor counselors?

3. What does it mean to have a multitude of counselors? Can you name some people you might go to for advice on buying a house? Choosing a career? Managing money? Rearing children?

Lesson Twelve

Happiness is a Choice

*Indeed, man wishes to be happy even when he so lives
as to make happiness impossible.* — *Augustine*

Lesson Goals
1. To learn that happiness is a choice
2. To examine the six decisions that bring happiness
3. To understand anger and its consequences

Happy or Angry?

Unless there is a radical change of direction, you will one day be what you are now becoming. The world is full of angry, bitter people. For most, their anger and bitterness began in their youth. If you really get them to open up to you concerning the root of their anger, it will not be very long before they will begin to blame some person or some circumstance in their past. However, what they may or may not understand is this: the decision to live your life angry or happy is a personal choice! It has nothing to do with what someone once did or something that once happened.

The book of Proverbs has much to say about happiness, a merry heart, anger, and the heart cancer of wrath.

Happiness is the Result of Six Personal Decisions

Happiness is not a goal, it is a by-product of being what you should be, and doing what you should do. It is the result of choices.

1. The Decision to Accept Jesus Christ as Saviour

Psalm 144:15, "Happy is that people, that is in such a case: yea, happy is that people, whose God is the LORD."

The joy of the Lord is only available to those who have made peace with God. We can only have peace with God through the shed blood of His Son, Jesus Christ. Salvation is a personal decision that produces great, personal happiness. To be a child of God is the greatest of all blessings! Are you saved?

(Teacher's note: Share your personal salvation testimony of how Jesus has changed your life!)

2. The Decision to Pursue Wisdom

Proverbs 3:13-18, "Happy is the man that findeth wisdom, and the man that getteth understanding.... She is a tree of life to them that lay hold upon her: and happy is every one that retaineth her."

The wisdom of God is contained in the Word of God. There are three ways God has given us to increase our knowledge of the Bible:

1) *Personal Devotions* – personally reading, memorizing and meditating on the Bible.

2) *Public Preaching* – listening with a teachable spirit to the preaching and teaching of the Bible.

3) *Private Counsel* – personally going to those who have good understanding of the Scriptures and asking them questions.

Wisdom insulates you against bad decisions. Poor choices bring regret and guilt and rob a man of joy and happiness.

3. The Decision to Trust the Lord

Proverbs 16:20, "He that handleth a matter wisely shall find good: and whoso trusteth in the LORD, happy is he."

Nothing destroys happiness like bitterness. Bad things are going to happen – it's just life. Not only are bad things going to happen, you are not always going to understand why they happen. It is easy to get bitter, if you do not learn to trust the Lord. Trust is necessary when you don't understand what God is doing. Trust is possible because you can understand who God is! God is good – all the time! You can trust Him.

Proverbs 3:5-6, "Trust in the LORD with all thine heart; and lean not unto thine own understanding. In all thy ways acknowledge him, and he shall direct thy paths."

4. The Decision to Live for Others

Proverbs 14:21, "He that despiseth his neighbour sinneth: but he that hath mercy on the poor, happy is he."

Another destroyer of happiness is selfishness. Happiness is a funny thing. If you pursue it for yourself, you never catch it. If you seek it for others, it catches you! The happiest people in the world are those who live for others.

If you can only be happy when someone is doing something for you, then your happiness is always controlled by others. If you can learn to be happy doing for others, then you can be happy anytime you choose.

5. The Decision to Maintain a Tender Heart

Proverbs 28:14, "Happy is the man that feareth alway: but he that hardeneth his heart shall fall into mischief."

The fear of the Lord keeps us tender to His working in our lives. When a young person begins to harden his heart toward the Word of God, he will soon discover that there is an unhappiness that comes with it. Fear always! Reverence God and His Word, and respond quickly to the voice of the Holy Spirit. A clean heart brings with it happiness.

6. The Decision to Live a Life Obedient to the Scriptures

Proverbs 29:18, "Where there is no vision, the people perish: but he that keepeth the law, happy is he."

Obeying the Bible brings happiness! Disobedience brings guilt, and guilt kills happiness. Obedience also brings blessings which in turn brings more happiness!

Why Are So Many Christian Teenagers Unhappy?

Many young people grow up in a good, Bible-preaching church but seem miserable. They think that the world will bring them happiness – after all, "I have been in church my whole life and I am not happy!" They rationalize that in order to be happy, they need to go out and try something else.

The cure for your unhappiness is NOT leaving church. The cure for your unhappiness is to begin to finally DO WHAT YOU ARE BEING TAUGHT TO DO IN CHURCH. Knowing what the Bible says to do and doing what the Bible says to do are two different things.

Are you unhappy as a Christian young person? If your answer is "yes," then answer these questions honestly:

- Are you really saved – *really* saved?

- Do you have a personal time with God's Word?
- Do you listen intently to the preaching and teaching of God's Word? Do you seek through private counsel to increase in wisdom? Do you actively seek the wisdom available in God's Word?
- Are you bitter over something that has happened that you do not understand? Are you willing to trust the Lord when you don't understand what He is doing in your life?
- Do you spend time every week living for others? Or are you focused on yourself?
- Do you have a tender heart? Are you responsive to the Holy Spirit's working in your life?
- Do you live a life of obedience to the Scriptures, or is your life marked by disobedience and uncon-fessed sin?

Every unhappy Christian is six decisions away from happiness.   Happiness is not the result of circumstances, but a result of the choices we make.

Happiness Produces a Merry Heart

Proverbs 15:13, "A merry heart maketh a cheerful countenance: but by sorrow of the heart the spirit is broken."

Proverbs 15:15, "All the days of the afflicted are evil: but he that is of a merry heart hath a continual feast."

Proverbs 17:22, "A merry heart doeth good like a medicine: but a broken spirit drieth the bones."

The result of making the right choices is happiness. The byproduct of happiness is a merry heart! A merry heart is like medicine to the body, a feast to the spirit, and an anointing to our countenance. It changes us inside, and this change affects our outward appearance. Being right with God, walking with God, being filled with His wisdom, living our lives for the good of others and the glory of God – all these things produce an inner happiness and peace that changes our heart for the better.

Disobedience, rebellion, and bitterness do just the opposite. These things bring sorrow, affliction, and, if allowed to run their course, will eventually break the spirit of a Christian.

Points to Ponder and Discuss

1. How would the decision to trust the Lord insulate you from bitterness?

2. What is the difference between the actions of others and your reaction to the actions of others?

3. Who are the happiest people at your church? Why?

Lesson Thirteen

Anger is a Choice

Anger is one letter short of danger. — Unknown

Lesson Goals
1. To understand that anger is a choice
2. To understand the consequences of anger
3. To understand the real cause of anger

Colossians 3:8, "But now ye also put off all these; anger, wrath, malice, blasphemy, filthy communication out of your mouth."

The Cancer of Anger

Young people who refuse to fear the Lord and obey the Bible soon find out that there are consequences for disobedience. They begin to lose the blessing of God upon their lives and begin to receive the chastening of the Lord instead. I cannot tell you how many times this leads to anger. As silly as it may sound, the average rebellious teenager harbors anger toward God for refusing to bless him in his disobedience and rebellion.

"How dare God expect me to play by His rules!"

Our culture is infected with an entitlement mentality! Too many young people believe that God owes them – that somehow God is supposed to open the windows of Heaven and pour out His blessings upon them despite their unwillingness to obey His Word.

Sadly, this wrath spills over on others. Soon, these teenagers become jealous toward those who are doing right, and being blessed for it. This jealously leads to bitterness, bitterness to anger, and anger unchecked leads to a multitude of problems in their lives.

The Consequences of Anger

People who are constantly angry have to understand that they do not have anger problems. Anger is a by-product, not a cause. If the root of the problem is not addressed, their anger soon begins to create other issues in their lives.

1. Unwise Decisions

Proverbs 14:17, "He that is soon angry dealeth foolishly: and a man of wicked devices is hated."

Ecclesiastes 7:9, "Be not hasty in thy spirit to be angry: for anger resteth in the bosom of fools."

Anger clouds our thinking. It is impossible to make good decisions while mad. Because of this, the angry man deals foolishly. His choices lack wisdom and, as a result, bring more problems into his life.

2. Isolation

Proverbs 21:19, "It is better to dwell in the wilderness, than with a contentious and an angry woman."

Proverbs 22:24, "Make no friendship with an angry man; and with a furious man thou shalt not go:"

The Bible commands wise men to avoid those who are filled with anger. No one wants to be with a person who constantly flies off the handle over things. Anger leads to isolation.

3. Strife and Cruelty

Proverbs 29:22, "An angry man stirreth up strife, and a furious man aboundeth in transgression."

Proverbs 30:33, "Surely the churning of milk bringeth forth butter, and the wringing of the nose bringeth forth blood: so the forcing of wrath bringeth forth strife."

Proverbs 27:4, "Wrath is cruel, and anger is outrageous; but who is able to stand before envy?"

"Wrath is cruel." Cruelty leads to strife. The world is only going to put up with your angry attitude so long. An angry person will be quick to argue, quick to fight, quick to mistreat those around him.

4. Punishment

Proverbs 19:19, "A man of great wrath shall suffer punishment: for if thou deliver him, yet thou must do it again."

Strife will eventually lead to punishment. Anger will sooner or later cause you to cross lines that society will not tolerate. Many a young man or young woman is sitting in prison tonight because of one moment of unbridled anger.

5. Heaviness

Proverbs 27:3, "A stone is heavy, and the sand weighty; but a fool's wrath is heavier than them both."

Carry a large stone for any distance. Then pick up a bag of sand and tote it awhile. Doing either is exhausting! A fool's wrath soon becomes a heavy burden – a burden upon the one filled with anger, and sadly, a burden for those who are forced to interact with him.

Isn't It Time to be Honest About the Real Problem?

Ephesians 4:31-32, "Let all bitterness, and wrath, and anger, and clamour, and evil speaking, be put away from you, with all malice: And be ye kind one to another, tenderhearted, forgiing one another, even as God for Christ's sake hath forgiven you."

The first sin listed in the above verses is bitterness. This is the number one source of anger. The quiet sin below the surface producing the wrath, anger, clamor, evil speaking and malice is bitterness.

What I am going to say next is important: ALL BITTERNESS IS BITTERNESS AGAINST GOD.

"No, preacher, you are wrong. I'm bitter because of something that happened to me." No you are not. You are bitter against God for letting it happen.

"No, I'm bitter because of what someone said or did to me." No, you are bitter against God for letting them do it or say it to you.

How dare God make life so unfair for you! Why doesn't God solve all your problems and remove all your trials?

You are clay on the potter's wheel, still being formed into the vessel the master needs it to be. The vessel cannot take shape without pressure. God allows things into every life that may not make sense at the time. During your teenage years, you are being prepared in ways you cannot begin to understand. Things are going to happen that seem unfair, and difficulties are going to arise that seem overwhelming.

When this happens, you have to make a choice. You will either get bitter at God, and become angry as a result, or you will choose to trust God. He loves you, and He knows what is best.

Points to Ponder and Discuss

1. Is anger the problem or the by-product of a bigger problem? Explain.

2. Share your thoughts on this statement, "All bitterness is bitterness against God."

3. What has happened in your life that causes you the most anger? Can you trust God enough to accept it as part of His will for your life? Can you see, in the future, a chance to use this negative in your life to help someone?

Lesson Fourteen

Teachable or Scorner?

*The Spirit, who inspired Holy Scripture, lives forever,
and He delights to open the Word to those who
seek His instruction.*
— Charles Spurgeon

Lesson Goals

1. Grasping the importance of receiving instruction
2. Learning the attributes of a scorner
3. Learning the consequences of scorning

The Greatest Ability is Teachability

Proverbs 13:1, "A wise son heareth his father's instruction: but a scorner heareth not rebuke."

Anyone who is willing to study the book of Proverbs with an open mind comes away convinced of this one thing: being teachable may be the most important quality a teenager can possess.

The Importance of Receiving Instruction

The book of Proverbs overflows with verses that tell us of the importance of being teachable! A man will choose to be teachable, or he will go the way of the scorner.

Remember, unless there is a radical change, you will one day be what you are now becoming. Where are you, right now, when it comes to your attitude toward instruction?

Proverbs 1:7, "The fear of the LORD is the beginning of knowledge: but fools despise wisdom and instruction."

Proverbs 1:8, "My son, hear the instruction of thy father, and forsake not the law of thy mother:"

Proverbs 4:13, "Take fast hold of instruction; let her not go: keep her; for she is thy life."

Proverbs 8:10, "Receive my instruction, and not silver; and knowledge rather than choice gold."

Proverbs 8:33, "Hear instruction, and be wise, and refuse it not."

Proverbs 9:9, "Give instruction to a wise man, and he will be yet wiser: teach a just man, and he will increase in learning."

Proverbs 10:17, "He is in the way of life that keepeth instruction: but he that refuseth reproof erreth."

Proverbs 12:1, "Whoso loveth instruction loveth knowledge: but he that hateth reproof is brutish."

Proverbs 13:1, "A wise son heareth his father's instruction: but a scorner heareth not rebuke."

Proverbs 13:18, "Poverty and shame shall be to him that refuseth instruction: but he that regardeth reproof shall be honoured."

Proverbs 15:5, "A fool despiseth his father's instruction: but he that regardeth reproof is prudent."

Proverbs 15:32, "He that refuseth instruction despiseth his own soul: but he that heareth reproof getteth understanding."

Proverbs 19:20, "Hear counsel, and receive instruction, that thou mayest be wise in thy latter end."

Proverbs 23:12, "Apply thine heart unto instruction, and thine ears to the words of knowledge."

Your Attitude Toward Instruction is Your Choice

The proper attitude toward instruction is vital to growing in grace. It is the path to knowledge, understanding, and wisdom. To despise (undervalue or disregard) instruction is to declare oneself a fool. Instruction is life and the way of life! The Scriptures tell us to value instruction above silver and gold. To refuse instruction will cause you to err, will turn you into a brute, will lead to poverty and shame, and will destroy your soul.

Worst of all, if an unteachable spirit is not corrected, one day it will turn you into a scorner.

The Attributes of the Scorner

Proverbs 24:9, "The thought of foolishness is sin: and the scorner is an abomination to men."

If you have begun to become unteachable, you have placed yourself in danger of one day becoming a scorner. As we will see, if someone embraces the role of a scorner, he becomes an abomination to man, and a direct target for divine judgment.

1. Who is a scorner?

A scorner, by definition, is one who publicly holds a

teaching authority (both the message and the messenger) in derision; one who vocally scoffs, vocally mocks, vocally imitates in mockery the teacher or preacher; one who mocks truth.

2. A scorner, sadly, at some point begins to delight in his role as a derider of truth.

He sees it as sport. He thinks that mocking a teacher or preacher and mocking their message makes him something special.

Proverbs 1:22, "How long, ye simple ones, will ye love simplicity? and the scorners delight in their scorning, and fools hate knowledge?"

Proverbs 10:23, "It is as sport to a fool to do mischief: but a man of understanding hath wisdom."

3. Scorning is an "armchair" activity.

Those who participate are good at sitting, but not known for actually doing much of anything. They know it all, but do nothing at all. Notice in the verse below the scorner is "sitting in the seat of the scornful." The "blessed" man refuses to participate in scorning.

Psalms 1:1, "Blessed is the man that walketh not in the counsel of the ungodly, nor standeth in the way of sinners, nor sitteth in the seat of the scornful."

The path to becoming a scorner starts by listening to the counsel of ungodly people, and by hanging around those callously involved in a sinful lifestyle.

4. A scorner soon becomes uncorrectable.

Every attempt to correct him, by those in authority over him, is perceived as a personal attack. Verbal reproof will not work with a scorner. Anyone who attempts to reprove him will be attacked and lied about. His hatred for instruction turns into a hatred for the instructors.

Sadly, in his mind, a scorner sees himself as right, authority as wrong, and there is no way of making him see otherwise. Reproving a scorner does no good because he will not heed reproof. Instead, he will be glad of it because it gives him further cause to publicly scorn those in authority.

Proverbs 9:7-8, "He that reproveth a scorner getteth to himself shame: and he that rebuketh a wicked man getteth himself a blot. Reprove not a scorner, lest he hate thee: rebuke a wise man, and he will love thee."

Proverbs 15:12, "A scorner loveth not one that reproveth him: neither will he go unto the wise."

Proverbs 13:1, "A wise son heareth his father's instruction: but a scorner heareth not rebuke."

5. A scorner must be punished.

Proverbs 21:11, "When the scorner is punished, the simple is made wise: and when the wise is instructed, he receiveth knowledge."

Proverbs 19:25, "Smite a scorner, and the simple will beware: and reprove one that hath understanding, and he will understand knowledge."

Ignoring a scorner will not solve the problem. Since they have proven they will not be corrected, there is nothing left to do but to punish them. This is not for their sake, but for the sake of those tempted to follow their example.

6. A scorner must be cast out.

Yes, they need to be banished. Kicked out. Removed. A Christian school that allows scorners to attend is breaking a command of God. The youth pastor who tolerates scorners is being disobedient to the Lord. A pastor who knowingly welcomes scorners into his congregation is a fool.

Proverbs 22:10, "Cast out the scorner, and contention shall go out; yea, strife and reproach shall cease."

A scorner who eventually has to be cast out should never be looked at as a victim. Remember, scorning is a choice. He chooses to scorn, but he can just as easily repent of that sin, change his attitude, and become teachable. If he refuses, then he must bear the consequences alone.

Proverbs 9:12, "If thou be wise, thou shalt be wise for thyself: but if thou scornest, thou alone shalt bear it."

Why does God insist on eliminating the scorner?

Proverbs 29:8, "Scornful men bring a city into a snare: but wise men turn away wrath."

If this is true of a city, then isn't it also true that scornful teens will eventually bring a youth group into a snare? Perhaps an entire church? Ignoring scorners will not solve the problem, it just allows them time to do more damage.

7. Since a scorner will not submit to the correction of earthly authority, God Himself steps in with direct and divine chastisement.

Proverbs 3:33, "The curse of the LORD is in the house of the wicked: but he blesseth the habitation of the just. Surely he scorneth the scorners: but he giveth grace unto the lowly."

Proverbs 19:29, "Judgments are prepared for scorners, and stripes for the back of fools."

God's Word is very specific when it comes to dealing with a full-blown scorner. Sadly, there comes a point when those in authority have no other option but to punish the scorner, cast out the scorner, and turn him over to the direct judgment of God. Scorning is not to be tolerated, accepted, or excused – it is to be punished. This is not for the sake of the scorner, but for the sake of the simple. Sadly, only God can get his attention. And God will.

Points to Ponder and Discuss

1. What is your attitude toward instruction?

2. When a young person turns into a full-blown scorner, is there any use rebuking him? Why?

3. What does God promise to do to the scorner in Proverbs 3:33? What do you think that means?

4. If those in authority have to cast out a scorner, why would it be wrong to view the scorner as a victim, and those in authority as uncaring and uncompassionate?

Lesson Fifteen

Prosperous or Poor?

The fellow that has no money is poor.
The fellow that has nothing but money is poorer still.
— Billy Sunday

Lesson Goals
1. To examine the causes of poverty
2. To examine the dangers of riches
3. To learn to have the proper view towards money and material possessions

Contrasting the Rich and the Poor

Proverbs 22:2, "The rich and poor meet together: the LORD is the maker of them all."

God does not judge a man's worth by dollars and cents. In this age, too much importance is put on materialism. Many have become obsessed with money and the things it can buy. Sadly, contentment is condemned and covetousness is congratulated! God does not view life in this way. He loves the poor the same as He does the rich – He is not a respecter of persons.

It is important that we understand that money is simply a tool – a necessary tool, but just a tool. It is a tool to be used, not a god to be worshipped. Poverty creates problems in our lives, but as we will see, riches can do the same! We are going to look at what the book of Proverbs has to say about prosperity and poverty.

Weak Character Can Contribute to a Man's Poverty

We will see, shortly, that not all poverty is produced by a lack of character. However, a lack of character certainly can produce poverty.

1. Laziness can contribute to poverty.

Proverbs 6:6-11, "Go to the ant, thou sluggard; consider her ways, and be wise: Which having no guide, overseer, or ruler, Provideth her meat in the summer, and gathereth her food in the harvest. How long wilt thou sleep, O sluggard? when wilt thou arise out of thy sleep? Yet a little sleep, a little slumber, a little folding of the hands to sleep: So shall thy poverty come as one that travelleth, and thy want as an armed man."

Proverbs 20:13, "Love not sleep, lest thou come to poverty; open thine eyes, and thou shalt be satisfied with bread."

2. Unethical business dealings will eventually produce poverty.

Proverbs 10:4, "He becometh poor that dealeth with a slack hand: but the hand of the diligent maketh rich."

Proverbs 28:8, "He that by usury and unjust gain increaseth his substance, he shall gather it for him that will pity the poor."

Many businessmen cheat and swindle others to get ahead financially. What they fail to realize is that their lives are in God's hands. God can control things that they cannot control. Ill-gotten gain is placed in bags full of holes. In the end, every man will reap what he has sown. The Bible says "he will gather it for him that will pity the poor."

3. An extravagant lifestyle and wasteful spending can produce poverty.

Proverbs 21:17, "He that loveth pleasure shall be a poor man: he that loveth wine and oil shall not be rich."

Proverbs 23:21, "For the drunkard and the glutton shall come to poverty: and drowsiness shall clothe a man with rags."

Proverbs 18:9, "He also that is slothful in his work is brother to him that is a great waster."

4. An unteachable spirit will lead to poverty.

Proverbs 13:18, "Poverty and shame shall be to him that refuseth instruction: but he that regardeth reproof shall be honoured."

Proverbs 22:4, "By humility and the fear of the LORD are riches, and honour, and life."

5. The desire to "get rich quick" will produce poverty.

Proverbs 28:22, "He that hasteth to be rich hath an evil eye, and considereth not that poverty shall come upon him."

A Christian Should Never Trust in His Riches

As born again believers, our trust must always be directed to the Lord! It is a dangerous thing to place your trust in riches. All that we have could be gone in an instant — ask Job! We are to be thankful for the things we have, but our trust must always be in God and God alone.

Proverbs 11:28, "He that trusteth in his riches shall fall: but the righteous shall flourish as a branch."

Proverbs 23:5, "Wilt thou set thine eyes upon that which is not? for riches certainly make themselves wings; they fly away as an eagle toward heaven."

Proverbs 27:24, "For riches are not for ever: and doth the crown endure to every generation?"

Many Good People Have Chosen Poverty in Exchange for Greater Riches

Proverbs 13:7, "There is that maketh himself rich, yet hath nothing: there is that maketh himself poor, yet hath great riches."

Be careful not to look down upon the poor – you may be looking down upon a king! Some of the choicest of God's servants have turned their back on the money and fame that they could very easily have attained and have exchanged it all for a chance to do God's work! Some of the brightest minds and hardest workers are living in near poverty as missionaries, pastors, assistant pastors, evangelists, and Christian school teachers. Some of these, of whom God said "the world was not worthy" (Hebrews 11:38), have even given their very lives!

God Gives Stern Warning to Those Who Would Despise or Mistreat the Poor!

God also promises blessings and benefits to those who show mercy to the poor. Young person, be very careful how you treat those less fortunate than yourself!

1. God sees the mistreatment of the poor as sin.

Proverbs 14:21, "He that despiseth his neighbour

sinneth: but he that hath mercy on the poor, happy is he."

If you look down on the poor, and have the viewpoint that they are not as important to God as you are, then God sees that as sin in your heart.

2. If you mistreat the poor, God takes it personally.

Proverbs 14:31, "He that oppresseth the poor reproacheth his Maker: but he that honoureth him hath mercy on the poor."

Proverbs 17:5, "Whoso mocketh the poor reproacheth his Maker: and he that is glad at calamities shall not be unpunished."

God takes the oppression and mistreatment of the poor seriously and personally. God takes it as a personal reproach. Be very careful how you treat the poor.

3. God rewards those who are kind to the poor.

Proverbs 19:17, "He that hath pity upon the poor lendeth unto the LORD; and that which he hath given will he pay him again."

Proverbs 21:13, "Whoso stoppeth his ears at the cry of the poor, he also shall cry himself, but shall not be heard."

Proverbs 22:9,16,22, "He that hath a bountiful eye shall be blessed; for he giveth of his bread to the poor...He that oppresseth the poor to increase his riches, and he that giveth to the rich, shall surely come to want...Rob not the poor, because he is poor: neither oppress the afflicted in the gate:"

When you help the poor, God notices. God will be debtor to no man. God rewards those who bless the poor.

So, is it Better to be Poor or Rich?

The Bible answer seems to be neither! Perhaps it is better to just be somewhere in between – and then decide to be content doing the will of God.

Proverbs 30:8-9, "Remove far from me vanity and lies: give me neither poverty nor riches; feed me with food convenient for me: Lest I be full, and deny thee, and say, Who is the LORD? or lest I be poor, and steal, and take the name of my God in vain."

Points to Ponder and Discuss

1. What does this statement mean to you? "Money is a tool to be used, not a god to be worshipped."

2. What does this statement mean to you? "Ill-gotten gain is placed in bags full of holes."

3. So, is it better to be poor or rich?

Lesson Sixteen

Blessed or Cursed?

*Our souls are immortal; and all crime will be punished,
and virtue rewarded, either here or hereafter.*
— *Benjamin Franklin*

Lesson Goals
1. To encourage you to do a word study on "blessed"
2. To encourage you to do a word study on "cursed"
3. To learn the secrets of the "blessed life"

It's Your Choice

Proper character secures providential blessings. There are many good reasons to improve your character, but one of the strongest ones is that God promises to bless those who do. One of the most beneficial Bible studies anyone can conduct is the study of the words "blessed" and "cursed." From this study you will learn that God blesses character. Wisdom, diligence, prudence, virtue, humility, teachability – all of these come with the promise of God's good grace.

So, you have to decide. Do you want to live blessed or cursed?

It is All about the Bible

Psalm 1:1-3, "Blessed is the man that walketh not in the counsel of the ungodly, nor standeth in the way of sin-

ners, nor sitteth in the seat of the scornful. But his delight is in the law of the LORD; and in his law doth he meditate day and night. And he shall be like a tree planted by the rivers of water, that bringeth forth his fruit in his season; his leaf also shall not wither; and whatsoever he doeth shall prosper."

Let's start where God starts. He has given us a Book. What we do with it determines His blessing upon us. More and more people in this culture choose to ignore its teachings. Some even blaspheme its truths.

Thank God for the handful who cherish the truths contained in the Scriptures. These are the blessed ones.

Psalm 119:1-2, "Blessed are the undefiled in the way, who walk in the law of the LORD. Blessed are they that keep his testimonies, and that seek him with the whole heart."

If You Are Saved, You are Blessed!

Psalm 32:1-2, "Blessed is he whose transgression is forgiven, whose sin is covered. Blessed is the man unto whom the LORD imputeth not iniquity, and in whose spirit there is no guile."

Your worst day on earth is heaven compared to hell. If you are saved, you are blessed. Thank God every day for your salvation.

Secrets to the Blessed Life

The secret of the blessed life is NOT a secret. God is very transparent with us. He clearly states in the Scriptures WHAT he will bless and WHAT he will curse. How can we be mad at God for keeping His word?

1. No matter what happens, NEVER stop trusting the Lord.

Psalm 2:12, "Kiss the Son, lest he be angry, and ye perish from the way, when his wrath is kindled but a little. Blessed are all they that put their trust in him."

Psalm 34:8, "O taste and see that the LORD is good: blessed is the man that trusteth in him."

Psalm 40:4, "Blessed is that man that maketh the LORD his trust, and respecteth not the proud, nor such as turn aside to lies."

Life is going to throw you some wicked curves. Some things will happen that you will not understand. Decide now that no matter what happens, you are going to trust the Lord.

Job did not understand what God allowed him to go through. He had to make a decision. Job could have gotten bitter, but then he would have missed the blessings God had for him down the road.

Proverbs 3:5-6, "Trust in the LORD with all thine heart; and lean not unto thine own understanding. In all thy ways acknowledge him, and he shall direct thy paths."

2. Look for someone to help.

Psalm 41:1, "Blessed is he that considereth the poor: the LORD will deliver him in time of trouble."

Proverbs 22:9, "He that hath a bountiful eye shall be blessed; for he giveth of his bread to the poor."

God takes care of those who take care of others.

One of the joys of life is helping those who cannot help themselves. A selfish person is cursed. And the sad thing is, he brings this curse upon himself. If you choose to live for others, your own personal happiness will increase dramatically.

3. When God chastens you – it is evidence of His love.

Psalm 94:12, "Blessed is the man whom thou chastenest, O LORD, and teachest him out of thy law;"

Hebrews 12:5-8, "And ye have forgotten the exhortation which speaketh unto you as unto children, My son, despise not thou the chastening of the Lord, nor faint when thou art rebuked of him: For whom the Lord loveth he chasteneth, and scourgeth every son whom he receiveth. If ye endure chastening, God dealeth with you as with sons; for what son is he whom the father chasteneth not? But if ye be without chastisement, whereof all are partakers, then are ye bastards, and not sons."

It is wonderful to be able to call God our Father! But sometimes we forget that part of a father's responsibility is to chastise his children. This is a blessing! God uses His gentle chastening to keep us in His will and to steer us away from harm. Chastisement is a proof of God's love!

4. Never lose your fear of the Lord.

Psalm 112:1, "Praise ye the LORD. Blessed is the man that feareth the LORD, that delighteth greatly in his commandments."

God blesses those who hold Him in respect. One of the great benefits of fearing the Lord is the promise of His blessing. God does not tolerate disrespect for long. One of the ten commandments warns us against using God's name in vain.

Exodus 20:7, "Thou shalt not take the name of the LORD thy God in vain; for the LORD will not hold him guiltless that taketh his name in vain."

A man who reveres God, praises His name, obeys His commands, and loves Him supremely will be divinely rewarded.

5. Do right. God blesses the righteous and curses the wicked.

Proverbs 3:33, "The curse of the LORD is in the house of the wicked: but he blesseth the habitation of the just."

Psalm 7:11, "God judgeth the righteous, and God is angry with the wicked every day."

This is God's way. God blesses those who strive every day to live a righteous life. The Bible says the Lord searches the earth looking for opportunity to bless the righteous.

2 Chronicles 16:9, "For the eyes of the LORD run to and fro throughout the whole earth, to shew himself strong in the behalf of them whose heart is perfect toward him..."

When you are faced with a tough choice, always ask yourself, "What is the right thing to do?" Every time you do right, you ensure the approval and blessing of God.

Can Christians Put Themselves Under a Curse?

Just as God promises blessings, He warns of curses. Yes, if a Christian chooses an action or attitude that God has promised to curse, then God will keep His promise. Here are a few of the curses Christians either ignorantly or purposefully live under.

1. To purposefully and knowingly disobey a direct command of God, and turn to serve another god brings upon you a curse.

Deuteronomy 11:26-28, "Behold, I set before you this day a blessing and a curse; A blessing, if ye obey the commandments of the LORD your God, which I command you this day: And a curse, if ye will not obey the commandments of the LORD your God, but turn aside out of the way which I command you this day, to go after other gods, which ye have not known."

2. If we fail to bless Israel, and instead curse God's chosen people, we bring upon ourselves a curse.

Genesis 12:1-3, "Now the LORD had said unto Abram, Get thee out of thy country, and from thy kindred, and from thy father's house, unto a land that I will shew thee: And I will make of thee a great nation, and I will bless thee, and make thy name great; and thou shalt be a blessing: And I will bless them that bless thee, and curse him that curseth thee: and in thee shall all families of the earth be blessed."

This is true for individuals as well as nations. A church that wants to experience God's blessings would be wise to support Gospel outreach to the Jews.

3. Refusing to tithe and bring offerings results in a financial curse.

Malachi 3:8-9, "Will a man rob God? Yet ye have robbed me. But ye say, Wherein have we robbed thee? In tithes and offerings. Ye are cursed with a curse: for ye have robbed me, even this whole nation."

There is much more the Bible has to say about these two words: blessed and cursed. You can study these words out for yourself. God has laid it out for us in His Word. He tells us exactly how to get God's blessings on our lives – and how to avoid living under a divine curse.

Points to Ponder and Discuss

1. What is the greatest blessing any man or woman can receive?

2. Is ignorance an excuse for not knowing what God says about being blessed and being cursed?

3. In light of Psalms 73, how should we respond when we see the wicked prosper and the righteous suffering loss?

Summary

Deuteronomy 30:19, "I call heaven and earth to record this day against you, that I have set before you life and death, blessing and cursing: therefore choose life, that both thou and thy seed may live:"

I occasionally hear a Christian teen from a godly home complain about not getting to make his or her own choices.

"I don't get to choose anything!"

That is not true. Every day, you choose between success and failure and between happiness and unhappiness. Every day, you choose your future by slowly becoming who you will one day be. You do so when you choose between Godly character or carnal immaturity. Which of these will you choose?

Simplicity, Foolishness, or Wisdom?

Laziness or Diligence?

Pride or Humility?

Virtue or Moral Strangeness?

Fear of God or Fear of Man?

Prudence or Haste?

Godly Counsel or Disappointment?

Happiness or Anger?

Teachable or Scorner?

Poverty or Prosperity?

Blessed or Cursed?

Remember, God cannot go against His Word. He keeps His promises. So, choose wisely. And may God bless you accordingly.

Coming soon...

A Teenager's Guide Series:

A Teenager's Guide to the Local New Testament Church

A Teenager's Guide to Relationships

A Teenager's Guide to Self-discipline & Organization

A Teenager's Guide to the Invisible Creation

A Teenager's Guide to Prophecy

A Teenager's Guide to Victorious Christian Thinking

A Teenager's Guide to Silent Killers & Besetting Sin

A Teenager's Guide to the Bible & Prayer

A Teenager's Guide to Spirituality

About the Author

Jerry Ross is the pastor of the Blessed Hope Baptist Church in Jasonville, Indiana. He and his wife, Sheryl, have served together in the Gospel ministry for over 30 years. In addition to pastoring and writing, Pastor Ross is a popular teen speaker, conference preacher and revivalist.

To order books by Jerry L. Ross

Go to the website: *www.stayinthecastle.com*

Phone: 812-665-4375

Write: Ultimate Goal Publications
4969 W County Road 1200 S
Jasonville, IN 47438